Research Methodologies for
Drama Education

Research Methodologies for Drama Education

edited by Judith Ackroyd

Trentham Books

Stoke on Trent, UK and Sterling, USA

Trentham Books Limited

Westview House	22883 Quicksilver Drive
734 London Road	Sterling
Oakhill	VA 20166-2012
Stoke on Trent	USA
Staffordshire	
England ST4 5NP	

First published 2006

British Library Cataloguing-in-Publication Data
A catalogue record for this book is available from the British Library

ISBN-13: 978-1-85856-323-7
ISBN-10: 1-85856-323-2

Cover photograph: Kate Dyer

Designed and typeset by Trentham Print Design Ltd, Chester and printed in Great Britain by Cromwell Press Ltd, Trowbridge.

Contents

Acknowledgements

I wish to thank the contributors for the roles they played in the International Drama in Education Research Institute held at University College Northampton in July 2003, as well as for their chapters in this text. They join me in thanking all those at the conference who participated in research groups (Research stations) creating the possibility of this book:

Hala Al-Yamini, Rubiya Ali Khan, Christopher Anderson, Yi-Man Au, Michael Balfour, Christina Barrager, Alice Bayliss, George Belliveau, Gavin Bolton, David Booth, Joanna Boulton, Pam Bowell, Claudette Bryanston, Penny Bundy, John Carroll, Teng-Yin Chang Yu-Mei Chang, Yung Ching Chang, Young-Ai Choi, Athanasia Choleva, Shiaoyuth Chou, Sally Cook, Mary Cooney, Pauline Cooney, Henriette Coppens, Mark Cremin, Edith Demas, Sarah-Jane Dickenson, Rachel Dickinson, Michael Finneran, Kathleen Gallagher, Lorenzo Garcia, Ambika Gopalakrishnan, Fleur Gregory, Sally Harris, Christine Hatton, Brian Heap, Colm Hefferon, Yueh-Yi Hsu, Lidwine Jessens, Chloe Keller, Andy Kempe, Vivienne Kerridge, Yuriko Kobayashi, Linda Lang, Chris Lawrence, Yun-Hee Lee, Philip Lortie, Sally Mackey, Alistair Martin-Smith, Mary Ellen Lowe, Laura McCammon, Debra McLauchlan, Catherine McNamara, Marie-Jeanne McNaughton, Carmen Medina, Carole Miller, Liz Mitchell, Augustine Chiu Yu Mok, Morag Morrison, Rosario Navarro, Helen Nicholson, Peter O'Connor, Cecily O'Neill, Carmel O'Sullivan, John O'Toole, Allan Owens, Glennaellen Pace, Simon Parry, Chandrika Patel, Glenn Pearce, Johnathan Pitches, Charis Polycarpou, Ross Prior, Geoff Readman, Juliana Saxton, Barbara Schaefer, Shifra Schonmann, Lilla Scott, Pam Shaw, Jack Chi-Yee Shu, Iain Smith, John Somers, Madonna Stinson, Trona Stokes, Elizabetta Ticco, Jo Trowsdale, Carrie Urbanic, Christine Warner, Gustave Weltek, and Charles Youngs

We are very grateful to Jonothan Neelands who was the workshops facilitator, and to the participants in the drama sessions who provided the subject of the research: Emily Bull, Sue Culverhouse, Richard Conlon, Ros Conlon, Caroline Healey, Naomi Lloyd, David Montgomery, Michelle Maudsley, John Newman, Jay Pecora, Michael Supple, Jeffrey Tan, and Clea Underwood

Gillian Klein, at Trentham deserves my special thanks for her patience when a new job interrupted the progress of this edition. To my post graduate students – I am so sorry that you didn't get the advantage of these chapters earlier!

Thanks to my mother-in-law for her amazing proof-reading skills to this project and to Christine Eggleton for her patient work on the manuscript.

As always I wish to acknowledge the support of the much cherished Andy, Toby and Rupert.

This book is dedicated to

Jonothan Neelands

for the influential work he has shared with practitioners all over the world through both public practice, keynote addresses and many publications, and particularly for generously giving us a research site at IDIERI,

and to

Philip Taylor

for the gift of IDIERI.

Introduction

Reading about research methodologies in the abstract is not always easy. We struggle to grasp how the theoretical or practical applications might be utilised in our own specific contexts in moving a research idea forward. This text aims to overcome the difficulty. Here the reader is invited to see how seven different research methodologies might be applied to researching the same sample of educational drama practice. In addition, each chapter explains the research methodology and places it in a broader context, provides ideas about how readers might utilise each in their own research projects and suggests further reading.

This collection arises from the International Drama in Education Research Institute (IDIERI) held at University College Northampton, at which all the delegates observed the same four drama sessions taught by Jonothan Neelands and then worked in Research Stations to apply a specific research methodology to understanding an aspect of that practice. Below is Neelands' brief description of each of the four sessions. The Research Methodology chapter writers were all Research Station leaders at the conference, invited because of their particular expertise and experience in different research methodologies. They explain the processes undertaken in their groups to examine with the reader the relationships between the theoretical implications of the methodologies and the practices they generate. The title of the conference, Destabilising Distinctions and Definitions, became highly significant in the Research Stations. You will find examples in the following pages, such as the conscious destabilising of notions of validity in research.

Although the specific site of inquiry involves drama sessions, most of the writers are engaged in cross arts activity and research, and two work in the fields of Dance and Literature. The text is relevant not only to drama education but to wider educational contexts and arts practices. It will be of interest to post graduate students preparing for their research projects and also to academic staff who have been working in one particular research mode and wish to develop their understanding of a broader range of methodologies.

A note on terms

Confusingly, the term *methodology* is sometimes used synonomously with method, merely giving it a somewhat grander image. But the term methodology sensitises us to the indissoluble link between techniques of investigation and assumptions about the nature of the world and how we know it. The term actually depicts distinct methods and their accompanying epistemological and ontological assumptions.

Grady, in Chapter 5, makes a distinction between *research methodology* (the theoretical questions that inform our research and how it is done) and *research methods* (the actual tools and techniques used to gather evidence, information and data). In a sense, then, we can construe methodology as theory plus method. So a feminist research methodology is obviously underpinned by feminist theory. However, it is important to note that while we can seemingly separate our understanding of methodology and methods, we cannot conceive that methods are neutral techniques which can be innocently used to generate understanding. The methods are selected according to that theoretical underpinning. So in a feminist research methodology, methods will be selected that support that theoretical standpoint. The researcher selects her methods – tools and techniques used to gather evidence, information and data – according to her epistemological and ontological assumptions. Some research methods will appear in the hands of different research methodologies, so we cannot always ascribe particular methods to particular methodologies. We continue to find that distinctions and definitions refuse to remain static and clear cut.

The site of inquiry – Neelands' drama sessions

The space in which the Neelands' sessions took place often crops up because it raises many questions about observation in research contexts. It was consciously and overtly an unrealistic context. A hundred and twenty delegates sat around the edges of a hexagonal dance studio. They made up two rows, some on chairs, most on benches. Observers could see observers as well as the practice – as you can see in the cover photograph. A camera ran on a tripod in the corner of the room. Neelands worked with fifteen participants in the large space remaining, sometimes on mats to define a smaller, more intimate place. Neelands has provided the following descriptions of the work:

Using this book: *The practical sessions*

In these sessions I tried to demonstrate what I consider to be good practice in the English model of drama teaching. Each session was 90 minutes long and I tried to treat these periods as if each were a separate lesson of that length. The English model is based on a more structured approach to planning, using a variety of dramatic conventions in addition to Teacher-in-Role, to develop work which has clearly defined artistic and social objectives. The drama work is likely to include both in role and out of role activity and also both presentational and representational modes of making and performing.

Session One: *Antigone* by Sophocles

Here I tried to model how dramatic conventions and simple performance techniques might be used to make a classical text and democratic performance tradition more accessible and relevant for young learners. The session emphasised the timelessness of the myth of Antigone and its relevance to events in Iraq, as well as to the ideas of democracy, theocracy and dictatorship. The session focused on the Prologue and understanding the back-story of the Oedipus myth through Teacher in Role, still images, discussion, ensemble performance, ritual theatre.

Session Two and Three: *The Composition* by Antonio Skarmeta

This session was based on a story set in Chile during the Pinochet era, in which the military try to trick a class of children into betraying their leftist parents by inviting them to write a composition entitled 'What my Family Does at Night'. The session focused on the role of the teacher in a fascist state and the kinds of dilemmas a liberal teacher might face; at the heart was the moral and political question of whether the teacher should sacrifice himself to protect his children or whether it is already too late for the teacher to do anything. The session used a variety of conventions to create the school, classroom and society in which the story is set and placed participants in the role of the teacher at the moment of greatest tension in the story.

Session Four: *Cleaning up the Neighbourhood*
This session was based on a newspaper story about a group of young men who beat a homeless man to death on the grounds that they were cleaning up the neighbourhood. This was the least planned and least structured session. It was also the only one pitched at an adult level – the others were originally designed for younger participants. The session focused on the shaping of the youths' identities and their relationship to their community. It was improvised/based on discussion during the session.

This text might be used as part of a research methods or methodology course. It outlines seven different research methodologies, providing a wealth of information about them and concrete examples of their practical use. New researchers might use the text to aid their considerations of the different options open to them. Some readers may wish to read specific chapters at certain times according to their interests.

The text is, however, engaging as one whole project. It does paint a fascinating picture of different energies at work with a shared focus. Philip Taylor's opening chapter introduces the context of the book, considering the extensive recent developments in writing on qualitative theory and how it might impact on arts and educational research practices. He includes some background to the International Drama in Education Research Institute that he himself began in 1995. His chapter provides an overview from which to consider the following chapters on research methodologies.

1

Power and Privilege: re-envisioning the qualitative research lens

Philip Taylor

A brief history of the International Drama in Education Research Institute (IDIERI)

The evolutionary time span of a formalised qualitative research agenda in the field of drama education has been a relatively short one. While drama as an interpretive medium sat well within a qualitative domain, advances in thinking about the various qualitative research lenses that can be applied to drama education have been recent. The last ten years has witnessed unprecedented development in writing on qualitative theory and how this theory translates to the drama educator. In this chapter I plan to tease out this writing further, how it relates to the IDIERI community and its implications for where further research might be heading.

Educational drama research has moved from a more general commitment to naturalistic inquiry and ethnographic approaches, to a study of action research, reflective praxis and classroom-based inquiry, to an interest in critical and emancipatory forms of scholarship, to more recent discussions of the post-modern condition and how interpretive acts are often aligned to the political. The latter has seen various critical social theories emerging where researchers expose the lenses through which they are interpreting the world.

Critical social theory exposes how our cultural, gendered, race and *queer* ideologies can often reinforce the dominant hegemony.

In recent times, there has been a blurring of genres, what has been referred to as an aesthetics of representation. Here, the investigator experiments with ways of telling the tale and explores evocative uses of vignettes, playscripts, and other literary forms (Ely, 1996, p169; Denzin and Lincoln, 2000, p4). This is a breakdown of the conventional research text which is a master narrative that conforms to conventional forms of academic writing.

New researchers entering the field can often find themselves caught within a variety of theoretical positions and research genres. Those who grew up in a tradition that promoted the story of educational life over the ideological perspectives powering it are now confronted by a myriad of often competing ideas:

> We confront a range of highly partisan but quite separate commitments-to feminism, Marxism, lesbian and gay activism, ethnic consciousness raising, and anti-colonialism, among others. Each group champions a vision of the good, and, by implication, those not participating in the effort are less than good and possibly obstructionist. (Gergen and Gergen, 2000, p1036)

At the first International Drama in Education Research Institute (IDIERI) in Australia (1995) a conversation began on the various research paradigms open to the drama education researcher: from the quasi-experimental design which quantifies and measures human achievement (Saldana with Wright, 1996) to historical and life history paradigms (Swortzell, 1996; O'Brien, 1996) to philosophical and aesthetic inquiry (O'Neill, 1996; O'Toole, 1996) and to the case study which celebrated teachers and their students' voices within an educational drama act (Edmiston and Wilhelm, 1996; Neelands, 1996; Taylor, 1996). Critical and emancipatory forms of inquiry were represented where participants were challenged to critique how their own positionality around a research act might reinforce privilege and marginalisation (Grady, 1996; Carroll, 1996). My reading of the presentations from the first IDIERI was that the field was embarking upon a good conversation about how research interfaced with drama education. However, questions related to how we exist in the world (ontological issues), and how we think in this world (epistemological issues) were on the sidelines rather that at the centre of this conversation.

There was never any intention that IDIERI would have a life following the 1995 meeting, but clearly the need for a continuation of international meetings where the drama education community gathered for discussion on research and scholarship was needed. The papers which emerged from the second institute, now with a title "The Research of Practice: The Practice of Research" demonstrated a continuing commitment to teacher-based research (Saxton and Miller, 1998). Examples of exemplary teaching practices were presented by leading drama educators (David Booth, Warwick Dobson, John Hughes, and Cecily O'Neill)[1] with a graduate student providing reflective responses. Dialogue was at the centre of this institute, a dialogue which aimed to investigate the principles of praxis powering a teacher-researcher, and how these principles could be applied in other educational contexts. As the conveners of this second institute argued:

> The conversations that took place at the University of Victoria in July, 1997, arose from the underlying premise of the organising committee that research activity and drama education must have immediate application within educational contexts, and that children are central in both our practice and our research. (Saxton and Miller, 1998, p5)

The notion that research must resonate with the world of schools grew from IDIERI's commitment to a process drama orientation which privileges a collaborative improvisational encounter informed by the pioneering praxis of Dorothy Heathcote. Nonetheless, it would be fair to argue that the history of drama education has been driven by a suspicion of researchers and research activity. The attitude that scholarship was located within a rarefied academic domain that bore no resemblance to what actually occurred in classrooms was a dominating one. Drama educators prided themselves on their practice, and those who wanted to theorise about such practice were seen as getting in the way of the real work.

Such attitudes were clearly apparent in the many conferences and seminars which focused upon the master teacher leading demonstration sessions usually with young children.[2] The conveners of the third IDIERI, Brian Edmiston, Patricia Encisco, Cecily O'Neill and Christine Warner, like their predecessors, Saxton and Miller in Canada, and myself in Australia, had all been influenced by Heathcote's work, and framed this third institute with the focus, 'Asking the Right Questions? Drama, Diversity, and Research'. Again, the Institute

3

had a series of teaching illustrations which served as a catalyst for dialogue but there was an important new element: a desire to critique the teaching examples from a critical social theory perspective. The presence of leading feminist authors Madeleine Grumet and Patti Lather weaved into the discourse a central concern with the underprivileged, the silenced, those in the margins of meaning.

The fourth IDIERI, from which the chapters in this collection emerge, built upon the work of the previous three. Situated in the tranquil surroundings of Northampton, England, this research institute was framed by the title, 'Destabilising Distinctions and Definitions'. The commitment to qualitative renderings of human affairs was continuing but a more thorough critique on the perspective of the researcher and how scholarly investigations are often shaped by the values which drive investigations. The institute was structured around research stations. Participants selected one research station from a total of six: Case Study, Critical Ethnography, Feminist Methodologies, Narrative Inquiry, Performance Ethnography, Post-Structuralist Performances. In their very titles we see a broadening of the traditional qualitative domain, from the standard case study and ethnography to an examination of how the research is framed and whose narrative is being prioritised in any research account.

So what does all of this work tell us about the evolution of the qualitative research paradigm in drama education? What are the pressing concerns of qualitative investigators? Where are the differences in thinking? And how has our thinking advanced over the years?

The Qualitative Mind

The field of cultural anthropology where the lone ethnographer would enter exotic locations, usually in remote communities, is where we attribute the beginnings of the qualitative mind. The work of Mead (1923/1960), Malinoswki (1967), Bateson (1972), and other formative anthropologists neatly characterises this work of the traditional researcher engaged in writing culture. Writing culture in traditional anthropology was loaded with a sense of the foreign, sometimes pejoratively described as the primitive.

In Mead's (1923) influential study, *Coming of Age in Samoa: A psychological study of primitive youth for Western Civilization*, we have the classic characteristics of the genre: a westernised individual travelling with notepad and pen to a faraway land. We conjure up images of the authoritative early twentieth-century white man, or woman, interacting with the savage mind. The term qualitative inquiry reflected this desire to capture, principally through written exposition, new phenomena. And the early ethnographers, referred to as field workers, seemed larger than life figures who went into and returned from the field with stories about strange people. The further the country was from the industrial cities, the more valued it was as a field setting.

The anthropologists' desire to write culture demonstrated a commitment to narrative forms of inquiry, where telling the tale of what was observed became the predominant means through which the data could live. Rather than measure up one culture against another, the anthropologist developed evocative narrative forms to recapture a lived experience, a case study. While we attribute to the Chicago School of Education in the 1920s and 1930s a formal interest in adapting this method of inquiry to urban school settings, in the field of drama education we do have earlier novelistic accounts of rich descriptions of classroom practice. Gavin Bolton's two influential books, *Drama as Education* (1984) and *Acting in Classroom Drama* (1998), outline many of the early pioneers in drama, like Harriet Findlay Johnson and Caldwell Cook. These early leaders developed theories of effective classroom practice based on immediate observations and analyses of their own work.

Cook's *The Play Way* (1917) is an absorbing read. We enter the vibrant world of the children he taught at the Perse School in early twentieth-century Cambridge. There is reverence in Cook's writing, familiar to the traditional cultural anthropologist, and his style reflects a special romantic spirit of the time, as noted in the following passage, quoted by Bolton, where Caldwell describes a teenager's portrayal of *Hamlet*:

> Hamlet began the scene with an air of assumed madness, snapping on the words in a high pitched voice. But with 'Come, come and sit you down,' his whole bearing changed to suit his altered purpose. He became outwardly calm, but spoke a tense voice full of restrained excitement. Just that voice, in fact, which so frightened the queen that she cried out on murder ... The boys all watching in breathless interest. No one moved in his seat ...A change from pathos in 'This was your husband,' to contempt in 'This is your husband' – no easy thing for a boy to express-was very effective, and the tone in 'Ha!

Have you eyes?' rose to a kind of shriek, which seemed to make clear once and for all that the madness of Hamlet was neither real madness nor assumed, but hysteria ...

The other boys (at the end of the scene) remained sitting and no one spoke a word. The atmosphere showed that no comment was needed, so I praised it as the finest piece of work I had ever seen in the school; and the class dispersed. (Caldwell in Bolton, 1998, p39)

While we can smile with bemusement at the sentimentality of these observations and others like them, they do reinforce a quality in this traditional form of cultural reconstruction. The readers put their faith in the interpretations and conclusions drawn, and are expected to believe in the power of the narrative to evoke a special world where amazing, almost sacred, things take place. Postmodern interpretations of the gendered references in the above example would be subject to critique today, as would the sweeping statements as to how the boys interacted with and responded to the material. Just because a writer describes a student's reaction as 'full of restrained excitement' or that the audience was 'watching in breathless interest' does not necessarily mean that readers will be convinced of the authenticity or accuracy of the claims. Early examples of drama education sessions like Cook's value the authority of the author's deductions and rarely give an insight of the classroom event through multiple perspectives and voices.

This form of evocative prose has been dominant in the qualitative literature in drama education. While Cook might not have likened himself to a researcher interested in novelistic accounts of human affairs, he certainly paved the way for a number of texts which employed rhetorical devices to recapture classroom events. Slade's *Child Drama* (1954), Wagner's *Dorothy Heathcote: Drama as a Learning Medium* (1979), Booth's *Story Drama* (1994), Winston's *Drama, Narrative and Moral Education* (1998), Wilhelm and Edmiston's *Imagining to Learn* (1998), even my own *Redcoats and Patriots* (1998), all privilege the authoritative narrator who endeavours to interpret a lived event and draw conclusions about that event so that others, in this instance drama educators, can benefit from reading the tale.

By qualitative research, we generally refer to the practice of investigating and interpreting a culture. And this practice has now been widely adopted in drama education research. Educators have found that the thick descriptions that qualitative research yields can help to thoroughly recapture the lived experience of leaders and participants when they encounter dramatic activity. Through reading those descriptions others can learn about educational phenomena and reflect on their ability to structure and implement significant drama experiences. (See the Manley and O'Neill 1997, and Wagner 1998 anthologies).

What these qualitative studies have in common is a commitment to a grounded, field-based or situated activity that locates an observer and a site in the world. Or, as Denzin and Lincoln (2000) argue, these activities share 'a set of interpretive, material practices that make the world visible.' So, as Cook describes his own teaching, he draws on his powers of observation and participation in the field to interpret culture. As Slade (1954) develops his theories on child drama, he documents numerous incidents from his own classroom life. When Wagner (1979) writes about Dorothy Heathcote's teaching, she is drawing on rich and detailed observations to present Heathcote's pedagogical style. In these instances, there is a dependence on substantial note-taking, logbook entries, interviewing data, and wherever possible, audio-visual and other technical devices to assist in interpreting what occurred in the field setting in an authentic way.

In recent years, however, a substantial critique of the qualitative mind has begun. Drawing largely on the discourse in post-modernism and post-structuralism, and the writings on gender, race relations, anti-imperialism, colonial disempowerment, Marxist and queer theories, new ideas have come to the surface and taken-for-granted assumptions in the qualitative domain have been widely contested. Questions about authenticity, trustworthiness and power and privilege have come to the forefront, and we now see this reflected in analyses of educational phenomena.

New Ideas

If a pattern of educational research in the last fifty years in drama education has been to privilege the qualitative researcher probing classroom phenomena, we are now witnessing a more critical commentary on the reliability of this research. Issues to do with validity and objectivity are now of concern and the conclusions or themes which draw researchers in are interrogated for all the hetero-normative assumptions they might raise.

It was perhaps the biting critique of Dorothy Heathcote's work by David Hornbrook (1989/98), followed by a number of rejoinders which built on feminist and other post-modernist writings, which has greatly transformed how we think about qualitative research. A special themed issue of the Australian drama education journal, NJ[3], titled 'New Paradigms in Drama Education' brought many of these issues to the surface. The editorial clearly marked the terrain of the journal's contributors:

> The impact of feminism on drama education has been slow to happen. This issue presents post-modern feminist scholarship as a new paradigm that is beginning to ask some difficult questions about taken-for-granted notions of 'good' practice and to offer new ways of approaching both teaching and learning in drama. (Hoepper and McLean, 1995, p1)

Powered by an idea that there is not one way of characterising the inner life of the individual, that the human identity is always a construct of gender, language, class, race and ethnicity, the ability to draw generalised meanings or universal understandings became problematic. Drama educators, for instance, who endeavored to talk about how males and females operated in their classes were challenged (Nicholson, 1995); or teachers who developed process dramas on mythological topics which did not contest the power or gendered relationships present in them were open to criticism (Fletcher, 1995). The new paradigm in drama education was arguing that what was previously acceptable is no longer, that every minute detail of a teacher's planning, and the curriculum assumptions informing that planning, were now open to question.

Critical theorists building on the work of social theorists like Foucault, Derrida and Habermas have challenged qualitative researchers to examine the ethical frameworks being reinforced during educational practices (see Kincheloe and McLaren, 2000). It is now claimed that mainstream research practices are generally implicated in the reproduction of systems of class, race, and gender oppression. So, for instance, a study of drama in the social studies classroom, which taught curriculum without questioning the dominant ideologies powering that curriculum, is scrutinised. When the only voices represented in historical reconstruction are those coming from the mainstream, of one gender, of a particular class and background, the critical theorists challenge us to consider issues of social justice, diversity and equity.

My account of eighteenth-century revolutionary society in Boston, and how drama helps students develop positions around that society, might well be challenged today on the basis that it potentially represents stereotypical images of American patriots and the British establishment, despite the fact that the improvisational work was endeavouring to shatter stereotypes (see Taylor, 1998). One's positionality, and the lens through which the work is observed, whether this be through a Marxist, queer, feminist, class, race, or religious lens, can often highlight gaps in one's research, or demonstrate how one voice might dominate another's.

This was apparent in the work Cecily O'Neill led in Australia with a group of teacher educators in the early 1990s. Working from the Selkie myth, O'Neill constructed a two day workshop where participants were implicated in episodes exploring the compromises and losses experienced as the female protagonist is forced by a young fisherman, named Patrick, to become his wife and mother to three children. One of the participants in this workshop was offended that O'Neill did not take an opportunity to use this drama work as a platform for a more considered account of how women are treated in society. During the final hours of the workshop she made her objections clear:

> My interjections were designed to 'make' the others recognise that the female victims of society are so often doubly victimised. Firstly they are raped and then held responsible for the assault or post rape and they are shunned by society as soiled. Furthermore, as a victim of Patrick's (masculinist) quest for ownership of property-in this case the seal woman-she then became a tool for the valuing of phallocentric moral codes which dictate the woman as subservient to her family. The activity provided an ideal platform for the interrogation of value systems constructed to appear natural, universal and objective. I was disappointed that this opportunity was missed. (Fletcher, in Taylor p40)

This critique led to an exchange around the drama education community on the extent to which educators unintentionally may promote and reinforce stereotypical values. Some thought O'Neill had opened up such an exploration given the pained longings the seal woman had toward her natural home, the sea, and to the human children she bore. Fletcher thought O'Neill had not gone far enough.

Other educators who have found the reflective theatre form that Dorothy Heathcote promoted valuable have been challenged for failing to critique the embedded hetero-normative values that might underpin the work (see Hornbrook, 1998). This has led to the challenge for researchers of drama education praxis to review the notions of homogeneity they might be unconsciously reinforcing. It is one thing to argue that a drama session led to a kind of radical transformation in the participants, it is quite another to critique and interpret the ethical systems that it promoted.

The crisis of representation
In searching for an authentic portrait of research activity, investigators have begun to explore non-linear modes of representing data. The standard conventional research paper, with its introduction and problem statement, review of literature, methodological approach, data findings, conclusions and recommendations, is now under scrutiny. Rhetorical criteria have now come into play with narratives, vignettes, playscripts, poems, performances, pictorial representations, pastiche and collage being entertained as important data presentation forms which can provide insight into a research act.

The postmodernists have argued that qualitative researchers can no longer capture the lived experience. What was previously believed true is now problematic. For instance, just because a majority of research participants might agree to the power of a given strategy, theme, or approach in a drama session, does not necessarily attest to such power holding in all circumstances. Research can fail to account for those in the margins who don't follow the mainstream, who have a different agenda, or who want to assert another perspective, or who are simply silent. The desire to reach a uniform perspective can distort the shifting and multiple ways in which the world can be constructed.

What does it mean when researchers commit to such terms as reliability and generalisability? Who makes determinations about the authenticity of a particular portrait of a drama experience? At the fourth IDIERI there appeared to be a real struggle to seek out ways to capture the 'other'. Rather than depend on the grand narratives that draw wide-ranging conclusions covering the complete class, there is recent interest in the localised situation where small scale theories respond to specific problems, questions and particular situations.

In Northampton, the work in performance ethnography was especially revealing. There were attempts to present and air data so that audiences could form their own conclusions, rather than be dictated to by the researcher through an academic paper. One such project, Ah-ssess, presented the complex, humorous and diverse perspectives of arts educators as they grapple with decisions about human progress and achievement. Informed by principles of leading American theatre practitioners, Eve Ensler (1988), Moises Kaufman (2001), and Anna Deveare Smith (1993), a research document was constructed, following interviews with selected informants. This data was then crafted into a 30 minute performance text where the voices of the research participants were exposed (see Taylor, 2004). These voices articulated the tensions often experienced by educators as they begin to make decisions about their students' academic attainment. A sense of teachers being the victim of a national standards movement which aims to quantify human experience was a theme. Yet these same teachers' contradictory desire to have rubrics by which they can evaluate their students' work was apparent. How does one measure an artistic experience via rubrics? How does one satisfy the need to report neatly on students' ability when working through an aesthetic domain? These are complex issues which do not have simple and tidy answers.

There have been other drama researchers interested in exploring ways of rendering their data through an arts-based medium (Saldaña, 1998; Sallis, 2003; Mienczakowski, 1997). In theatricalising the data, and making aesthetic choices on form and content, these researchers endeavour to achieve a more transactional response from their audience. Readers aren't just receiving knowledge from a research report; they are constructing their own understandings based on their experience of the data. This fits well within the post-structuralist stance that interpretation is powered by the cultural, socio-political, gendered, ethnic and sexual lens through which the world is perceived. 'No pristine interpretation exists,' argue Kincheloe and McLaren (2000), 'no methodology, social or educational theory, or discursive form can claim a privileged position that enables the production of authoritative knowledge.' (p286)

By embracing the artistic medium as a way of re-envisioning the data, researchers acknowledge that qualitative research is a human-situated act, and that there is no one grand narrative that should hold priority. In heightening the reader or audience member's ability to construct their own interpretation of the data, there is promotion of the individual's capacity for freedom. Here, we find an aspiration in drama education scholarship for a truly democratic encounter where there is a blurring between the boundaries of the research and the researched, or a destabilising of the familiar definitions and distinctions of what research should entail.

While it is difficult to foretell a future, the Northampton IDIERI invited critical debate on data representation. The days of promoting one form of qualitative inquiry over another seem to have passed. If there is a new movement, it is powered by the desire for multi-textual approaches in research design. There is respect for the incomplete picture. Notions of expertise and authoritative viewpoints have been relegated to the margins, and the need for a pluralistic approach begins to be tolerated.

My reading of the fourth IDIERI was that a research narrative can become satisfying when it recognises that there are multiple positions and stances around any given event. Researchers need to struggle with the many perspectives and voices while acknowledging the contradictory tensions that often power the human experience. When engaged in such a struggle researchers demonstrate their own humanity and their capacity to commit to a re-envisioning of what qualitative inquiry can achieve in our field.

Notes

1   See the Saxton and Miller collection for descriptions of this work.

2   Dorothy Heathcote developed the demonstration session as a professional development tool for pre- and in-service teachers. See Bolton 2003.

3   NJ refers to the National Association for Drama in Education (NADIE) Journal. This Australian professional association is now known as Drama Australia.

References

Bateson, G. (1972) *Steps to an ecology of mind*, New York, Ballantine

Bolton, G. (2003) *The Dorothy Heathcote Story: biography of a remarkable drama teacher*, Stoke on Trent, Trentham

Bolton, G. (1998) *Acting in Classroom Drama*, Stoke on Trent, Trentham

Bolton, G. (1984) *Drama as Education*, Harlow, Longman

Booth, D. (1994) *Story Drama*, Ontario, Pembroke

Carroll, J. (1996) Escaping the Information Abattoir: Critical and Transformative Research (p.72-84), in Taylor, P. (ed) *Researching Drama and Arts Education: Paradigms and Possibilities*, London, Falmer

Cook, C. H. (1917) *The Play Way: An Essay in Educational Method*, London, Heinemann

Denzin, N. and Lincoln, Y. (2000) *Handbook of Qualitative research*, 2nd edition, Thousand Oaks: Sage

Edmiston, B. and Wilhelm, J. (1996) Playing in different keys: Research notes for action researchers and reflective drama practitioners (pp.85-96), in Taylor, P. (ed) *Researching Drama and Arts Education: Paradigms and Possibilities*, London, Falmer

Ely, M. (1996) Light the Lights! Research Writing to Communicate, in Taylor, P. *Researching Drama and Arts Education: Paradigms and Possibilities*, (pp.167-186) London, Falmer

Ensler, E. (1988) *The Vagina Monologues*, NY, Villard

Fletcher, H. (1995) Retrieving the Mother/Other from the Myth and Margins of O'Neill's Seal Wife Drama, NJ, 19:2, 25-38

Gergen, M. and K. (2000) Qualitative Inquiry: Tensions and Transformations, in Denzin, N, and Lincoln, Y. *Handbook of Qualitative Research*, (pp.1025-1046) Thousand Oaks: Sage

Grady, S. (1996) Toward a Practice of Theory in Practice (pp.59-71), in Taylor, P. (ed) *Researching Drama and Arts Education: Paradigms and Possibilities*, London, Falmer

Hoepper, C. and McLean, J. (1995) Editorial, *NJ*, National Journal of Drama Australia, 19:2, 1-2

Hornbrook, D. (1989/1998) *Education and Dramatic Art*, 2nd edition, London, Routledge

Kaufman, M. (2001) *The Laramie Project*, NY, Vintage Books

Kincheloe, J. and McLaren, P. (2000) Rethinking Critical Theory and Qualitative Research, in Denzin, N, and Lincoln, Y. *Handbook of Qualitative Research*, (pp.279-314) Thousand Oaks: Sage

Malinowski, B. (1967) *A diary in the strict sense of the term*, New York, Harcourt, Brace and World

Manley, A. and O'Neill, C. (1997) *Dreamseekers: Creative Approaches to the African American Heritage*, Portsmouth, Heinemann

Mead, M. (1960) *Coming of Age in Samoa: A psychological study of primitive youth for Western Civilization*, New York, Mentor (Original Work Published 1928)

Mienczakowski, J. (1997) Theatre of Change, *Research in Drama Education*, 2:2, 159-172

Neelands, J. (1996) Reflections from an Ivory Tower: Towards an Interactive Research Paradigm (pp.156-166) , in Taylor, P. (ed) *Researching Drama and Arts Education: Paradigms and Possibilities*, London, Falmer.

Nicholson, H. (1995) Drama education, gender and identity, *Forum of Education*, Faculty of Education, University of Sydney, 50:2, 28-37

O'Brien, A. (1996) Restoring our Dramatic Past (pp.105-114), in Taylor, P. (ed) *Researching Drama and Arts Education: Paradigms and Possibilities*, London, Falmer

O'Neill, C. (1996) Into the Labyrinth: Theory and Research in Drama, in Taylor, P. (ed) *Researching Drama and Arts Education: Paradigms and Possibilities*, London, Falmer

O'Toole, J. (1996) Art in Scholarship and Scholarship in Art: Towards a Poetics of Drama Research (pp.147-155), in Taylor, P. (ed) *Researching Drama and Arts Education: Paradigms and Possibilities*, London, Falmer

Saldaña, J. (1998) Ethical Issues in an Ethnographic Performance Text: the 'dramatic impact' of 'juicy stuff', *Research in Drama Education*, 3:2, 181-196

Saldaña, J. with Wright, L. (1996) An overview of experimental research principles for studies in drama and theatre for youth, in Taylor, P. (ed) *Researching Drama and Arts Education: Paradigms and Possibilities*, London, Falmer

Sallis, R. (2003) Ethnographic Performance in an All-Boys School, *NJ*, 27:2, 65-78

Saxton, J. and Miller, C. (1998) *The Research of Practice: The Practice of Research Victoria*, B.C., IDEA Publications

Slade, P. (1954) *Child Drama*, London, University of London Press

Swortzell, L. (1996) History as drama/Drama as History: The case for historical reconstruction as a research paradigm (pp.97-104), in Taylor, P. (ed) *Researching Drama and Arts Education: Paradigms and Possibilities*, London, Falmer

Smith, A.D. (1993) *Fires in the Mirror*, New York, NY, Anchor Books, 1993

Taylor, P. (2004) Qualitative Modes of Representation, *Drama Research*, Volume 3, 19:30

Taylor, P. (1998) *Redcoats and Patriots: Reflective practice in drama and social studies*, Portsmouth, Heinemann

Taylor, P. (Ed)(1996) *Researching Drama and Arts Education: Paradigms and Possibilities*, London, Falmer

Wagner, B.J. (1998) *Educational Drama and Language Arts: What Research Shows*, Portsmouth, Heinemann

Wagner, B.J. (1979) *Dorothy Heathcote: Drama as a Learning Medium*, London, Hutchinson

Wilhelm, J. and Edmiston, B. (1998) *Imagining to Learn: Inquiry, Ethics and Integration through Drama*, Portsmouth, New Hampshire

2

Re-imaging the Reflective Practitioner: towards a philosophy of critical praxis

Jonothan Neelands

The first day that we met, you know I had got the impression that there would be a few people looking in. You know when somebody asked well how many people will be watching the session and you said oh about 160 and I was waiting for you to laugh or for somebody else in the group to laugh and nobody laughed and that panicked me[1].

JN: How can we best model process when there is a critical audience observing? What is the gap between the participants' subjective experience of the process and the observer's perceptions of the experience from the outside?

Researching from the inside

During the IDIERI I was the teacher of daily sessions, which were observed by an audience of educational researchers. These sessions provided the material for research stations each of which was pre-occupied with the ethical, theoretical and practical problems of creating a relationship between the researchers as observers of practice, the practice and the teacher. In this sense, the pre-occupations of IDEIRI were to do with making meaningful sense of the experience of observing the practice from the outside. As the teacher, together with the students who formed my class, our pre-occupations were with making meaningful sense of our experiences on the inside of the teaching and learning. Our insider positioning was significantly different from that of the outsiders.

> We are the ones doing it not them
>
> **JN**: What ground rules are needed to protect the participants and to shift the observers from a critical audience perspective? Who has the power in this relationship and how might power relationships, if they exist, be equalised?

Consequently, the chapters in this collection outline the characteristics of a diverse range of theoretical and methodological positions occupied by educational researchers. This chapter promises something different and yet also something in common with the rest of the collection. What is different is that the reflective practitioner position describes a particular self-orientation towards understanding and improving one's own practice rather than towards the research of practice by external researchers. What is common is a shared commitment to the central emancipatory struggle of critical theory and practice, which will resonate with the descriptions of critical theory-based paradigms of research contained in the other chapters in this collection.

In most cases, research activity in schools, or in relation to schools, is temporally defined and executed. Researchers negotiate a period of time and a problem or phenomenon to research, with outcomes based on the analysis of findings during the period of research. In this sense much of the literature is concerned with the initiation, design, procedure and reporting of more or less closed case studies or instances. The literature also tends to focus on the ethical problems of building reliable, rigorous and truthful interpretive frameworks and the making of generalisations based on the observation and inquiry into practice led not by the researcher but by others.

Yes, that's right. It's the process of the week. I mean a lot of people are seeing it as that morning and not seeing that morning in relation to the morning before, and the morning afterwards which is the whole thing you know. And I think that's so important that you have got to see it as the whole week.

Jon one thing I would like to say is that I think the researchers that are criticising and saying that it should start with pretext and then go to free form. I would like to challenge any one of them to come in here and do the same thing.

JN: How does orthodoxy work against innovation in research, in inspection, in accountability to the system? How does/should a teacher respond to being told they are doing it wrong by authoritative researchers – how does this change the power relationship? What is the role of the external researcher in critical and emancipatory reflective practice?

Reflective practice, on the other hand, is a way of life; it is not bounded in the same way as outsider models of research. It refers to the nurturing and development of life- long dispositions and the ongoing and continuous self-inquiry into one's own professional practice (Taylor, 2000). The reflective practitioner does not bracket off episodes of practice for scrutiny, rather s/he continuously and persistently scrutinises practice on a daily basis across a professional life-time. In order to be effective the reflective practitioner strives to be self-knowing as well as other-knowing. To dig deep into self in order to bring into consciousness, the otherwise unconscious instincts, habits, values and learnt behaviours that shape their practice, as well as to self-distance their interpretations of the effects of self-as-teacher on the lives, achievements, experiences and aspirations of those they work with, both colleagues and students.

Jonothan, part of what I was looking at was in my way of teaching. What I try to do is find a balance between necessary constraint and structure and freedom and I am not sure I always get there. Can you talk about that? It was interesting you saying that the last day it was our work for instance. Can you just talk about that a little bit? Was it too tight the rest of the week, was it right, did it bother you – you know how did you feel about that?

> **JN**: What is the teacher's responsibility in process drama? What is the best way of striking a balance between necessary constraints required in all artistic work and necessary freedoms giving voice and choice? How is this balance influenced by current power/ knowledge equations and the desire to share both power and knowledge? How do I ensure that my work is progressively challenging so that there is a movement, over time, from teacher-led work to individual or group autonomy?

There is both a level of intimacy and of challenge to the very person-hood of the teacher implied in reflective practice, which makes it qualitatively different from other outsider paradigms of educational research. The external researcher tries to find truthful ways of looking through the window of rooms occupied by teachers and learners, the reflective practitioner looks instead for the most effective and ethical ways of living in the room with other teachers and learners. It is an essentially collaborative project, which seeks to combine the insider perspectives of learners and a collegiate of teachers working in the same locus as the reflective practitioner. The reflective practitioner dwells in the room before and after the researcher is privy to their practice.

> There are two things in particular I will be taking away and one is just a reminder of the unbelievable power of working in a group to forge relationships and friendships. I mean that's just striking to me how this group came together and, you know, the support that was there.
>
> **JN**: What is the relationship between the personal and social and the artistic in drama work? How can socially created artistic work be used to develop a critically conscious and effective ensemble or collective? Do these expressions of the social value of the work reflect the existential tension between the us and them identities of the audience and the participants?

Reflective and reflexive practice

For the purposes of this chapter then, a reflective practitioner is both a professional practitioner, in our case an arts educator, and also a practitioner of reflective practice. What I am suggesting is that the term reflective practitioner describes a working, practicing, professional who brings to their work a praxis (Taylor, 2000) shaped by reflection-on-practice and reflexivity-in-practice. They reflect on and consequently, or simultaneously, modify their professional practice and their professional practice is itself reflexive in terms of the transparency of the processes of selection, reflection and modification that underpin it.

This view incorporates the three dynamic concepts of Schon's classical model of reflective practice (1987):

> Knowing-in-action, the professional know-how which informs professional actions and interactions – the ways in which training and other sources of practical, professional, existential and theoretical knowing become or inform our practice, our behaviours, our mediations of classroom experiences.

> Reflection-on-action, the evaluation, or contemplation, of practice in terms of thinking back on our knowing-in-action in order to assess its efficacy or to consider changes in our practice which might lead to greater efficacy.

> Reflection-in-action, at its simplest refers to the thinking on our feet, during rather than after teaching episodes, which characterises all professional practice that is ethical and action-centred. It is a vital characteristic of arts education practice, particularly in those forms of drama education – sometimes referred to as process drama – which are co-operative, improvised, indeterminate and interactive. (O'Neill, 1995; O'Toole, 1992; Taylor, 2000)

The idea of reflexivity-in-practice brings an additional ethical dimension to Shon's model which stresses an active commitment to articulating and making visible the essential dialectic within teaching and learning processes and within/between the experiences of teachers and learners and others who are directly or indirectly effected by these experiences (Freire, 1998).

It presupposes, for instance, that there are systematic opportunities for dialogue about the processes and interpretations of teaching and learning between teachers, learners and others involved (for instance parents, colleagues, policy makers) and that these dialogues will shape the reflection on, and the interpretation and modification of, the on-going practice. This in turn assumes an ethical position based on the moral necessity of nurturing and formalising a partnership of voices in the classroom which is, in Britzman's words, 'sensitive to representing the voices of those experiencing educational life as sources of knowledge, and.... committed to preserving their dignity and struggle' (1991, p 52).

> Because we together, we knew what it was like, it was like our thing that we experienced together and other people was watching that.
>
> **JN**: Is this giving primacy to privatised experiences (the truth within rather than a truth established through dialogue with others)? How do we negotiate the differences between external and internal perceptions of what is going on? How do we both critically challenge our own world view whilst also insisting on our right to assert the authenticity of our own lived experiences?

It also presupposes that this kind of partnership-based reflection is itself concretely reflected in the words and actions of the teacher, at the level of knowing-in-action. In this way, reflective practice becomes embedded in a dialogic pedagogic practice so that every lived classroom encounter resonates with the possibility for renegotiation between teachers and learners, between theory and practice, between the contents of the planned curriculum and our own lived and local knowledges.

> When we live our lives with the authenticity demanded by the practice of teaching that is also learning and learning that is also teaching, we are participating in a total experience that is simultaneously directive, political, ideological, gnostic, pedagogical, aesthetic, and ethical. In this experience the beautiful, the decent and the serious form a circle with hands joined. (Freire, 1998, p 31-32)

In Western dramaturgy, reflexivity in performance is used to describe performances, which consciously disrupt the illusion of an immutable reality in both the means and meanings of theatrical representation. In Brecht's reflexive aesthetics for example, both the means and meanings of the production are transparently revealed as provisional constructions which cause us to reflect on the unfinishedness of the world rather than to passively and uncritically accept the versions of reality conveyed in the theatrical performance. In the same way, reflexive teaching, based on reflective practice, is designed to disrupt the natural authority of the teacher and the versions of reality contained in the curriculum plan, so that both teachers and learners are made aware of knowledge as an inter-active process which is selective, produced and constructed between teachers and learners rather than as the mechanical transference of naturalised and un-contestable facts and figures. In the same way I have used the students' voices as interruptions in this otherwise theoretical text, to break the flow much in the same way as Brecht used songs, narrations and music to break the reality of the play's narrative realism. Reflexivity in performance, which is intended to provoke a critical consciousness in the audience, is analogous to Frierian pedagogy in which:

> ...to teach cannot be reduced to a superficial or externalised contact with the object or its content but extends to the production of the conditions in which critical learning is possible.....In these conditions, those who are engaged in critical learning know that their teachers are continuously in the process of acquiring new knowledge and that this new knowledge cannot simply be transferred to them, the learners. At the same time, in the context of true learning, the learners will be engaged in a continuous transformation through which they become authentic subjects of the construction and reconstruction of what is being taught, side by side with the teacher, who is equally subject to the same process. (*ibid* p 33)

The critical theory model of reflective practice

John Dewey formulated one of the earliest references to reflective practice in modern educational discourse. He defined it as:

> Active, persistent, and careful consideration of any belief or sup-posed form of knowledge in the light of the grounds that support it, and the further conclusions to which it tends, constitutes reflective thought. (1933, p 9)

There are several features of this definition, which begin to outline some of the paradigmatics of a Reflective Practice. 'Active' is con-sistent with Dewey's pre-occupations with action-orientated and heuristic learning in social contexts; the emphasis is on creating a praxis in which professional actions are shaped at pedagogic, epis-temological and ethical levels by critical reflection and scrutiny of the assumptions underpinning both the normative methods of teaching and the knowledge which constitutes the content or field of instruc-tion. 'Persistent' refers to the necessity of embedding a critically conscious and reflective pre-disposition in all teaching and learning practices rather than isolating occasional opportunities for evaluation and feedback. 'Careful consideration' refers to a pre-disposition for what Freire terms 'methodological rigour' and 'research' (1988, p34), so that there is a constant questioning and testing of the common sense assumptions and other interpretations underpinning the pedagogic and epistemological dimensions of learning. This questioning and testing in turn leads to the shaping of new insights, or 'further conclusions', which inform the on-going development of an evolving and transforming live(d) curriculum (Aoki, 1996).

Can I just say I don't think I would have been able to have been as free as I was in the final lesson if you hadn't done the whole run up. In fact when I was in Antigone in the first class we did.. I volunteered to be Antigone without knowing the story or what I was doing..I felt you really, really assured me in that, because you could sense I wasn't 100% sure what I was supposed to do or what my views were as Antigone. And because you assured me in that later on in the week once I sort of expressed myself a little bit more, knowing that if I did go off at a tangent and go in the wrong way that you would some how manage to bring me back down to the base level. So I definitely think that we needed that run up to get where we were. So although I think people are talking about structures per lesson I think it's also the structure of the week as a whole.

JN: What are the roots of this defensiveness, of this sense of being misunderstood/misrepresented by the external researchers? What does it mean in practice to be a critical facilitator, who provides both support and challenge in social and artistic domains? Is this evidence of a supportive facilitator, or a protective one? What is the most effective way of analysing the cumulative experience, or progression, of the process over time rather than focusing on isolated episodes?

The roots of radical reflective practice and reflexivity are most evident in the critical theory and social science of Jurgen Habermas (1971, 1972, 1974). Critical theory is, in J. M. Bernstein's description:

> a tradition of thought that, in part at least, takes its cue from its opposition to the wrongs and ills of modern societies on the one hand, and the forms of theorising that simply go along with or seek to legitimise those societies on the other hand. (1995, p 11)

The critical theory position is founded in the belief that:

> ...the all-pervading influence of positivism has resulted in a wide-spread growth of instrumental rationality and a tendency to see all practical problems as technical issues. This has created the illusion of an objective reality over which the individual has no control, and hence to a decline in the capacity of individuals to reflect upon their own situations and change them through their own actions. (Carr and Kemmis, 1986, p 130)

Critical theory presupposes that both positivism and scientism seek to reduce essentially human and practical problems to a technical level in which spurious claims to scientific objectivity are used to mask, conserve and naturalise both the power of the powerful and the powerlessness of the powerless (Carr and Kemmis, 1986, p86). In other words problematic situations in education, such as low levels of literacy or the under-achievements of certain groups, are treated scientifically as if they were natural phenomena rather than as essentially problematic social-political constructions. By focusing on the technical level of description and analysis, positivist approaches serve to mask the reality that:

> It is probably cultural inertia which still makes us see education in terms of the ideology of the school as a liberating force and as a means of increasing social mobility, even when the indications tend to be that it is in fact one of the most effective means of perpetuating the existing social pattern, as it both provides an apparent justification for social inequalities and gives recognition to the cultural heritage, that is, to a social gift treated as a natural one. (Bourdieu, 1974, p 32)

The critical theory take on reflective practice, therefore, is shaped around the principle that knowledge and its selection are neither neutral nor innocent (Habermas, 1972). In this sense, the purpose of critical reflective practice is to:

> ...expose the operation of power and to bring about social justice as domination and repression act to prevent the full existential realisation of individual and social freedoms. (Habermas, 1979, p 14)

Reflective practice as an emancipatory project

For critical theorists, reflective practice is an emancipatory project, a process of enlightenment (Habermas, 1979), which seeks to empower teachers as agents of social change engaged in a process of first exposing and then, through their own politicisation and agency, moving from an authoritarian and elitist model of schooling towards a social democratic model. In Habermas' reasoning school knowledge and knowledge about schooling based on research are essentially problematic and serve different cognitive and social interests, which he broadly characterises as:

1. Technical: which characterises positivist methods of research which generate laws, rules, predictions and control mechanisms based on passive research objects.

2. Practical: which characterises hermeneutic, interpretative methodologies which seek to understand and make sense of human situations through the perceptions and the socio-culturally constructed and situated utterances of those involved – the participants themselves are seen as active subjects rather than passive objects of research.

3. Emancipatory: is concerned with praxis, defined by Kinchloe as action based on reflection with the intention of serving an emancipatory interest (Kinchloe, 1991, p 77).

These levels are accumulative rather than distinctive. In other words, emancipatory knowledge contains both technical and practical knowledge but goes beyond these other levels of interest.

In terms of drama teaching and the knowledge interests it serves, Habermas' schema can be represented as:

Technical

At this level, problems are reduced to the parameters of subject specific knowledge and the basic technical skills of classroom planning, management and assessment of pupils subject specific learning. The concept of subject and its parameters are not problematised. A typical research problem might be concerned with planning and implementing modifications to curriculum, pedagogy and assessment required by changes in an examination syllabus or National Curriculum order.

Practical

At this level teachers are concerned with trying to consider the needs and experiences of their students and how to modify teaching and learning in order to match the curriculum to local needs and learning styles. The technical problem outlined above is now further investigated by trying to build a hermeneutic based on an interpretation of the lives and cultures of the students. A typical problem might be identifying students who are at a crucial grade threshold and trying to understand how best to help them to achieve a higher grade.

Emancipatory

At this level teachers and their students critique the practical and technical levels. The teachers problematise the curriculum in terms of what and whose knowledge is valued and in terms of how inclusive and equitable the curriculum is for students who do not belong to the culture of power. A typical problem might be to identify a praxis, which will provide all students with equal access to privileged cultural knowledge and capital, whilst also ensuring that the boundaries of what is taught and how it is taught, extend to include knowledge and experiences which are inclusive and representative of the student's lived experiences. The purpose is to equip students both with the knowledge needed to be powerful and a critical consciousness of how power operates in the curriculum selection and beyond.

An emancipatory praxis, or action, is intended not merely to understand how participants construct their worlds but also to propose ways in which the patterns of power, which regulate their worlds, might be changed. How, Habermas asks, 'Can we obtain clarification of what is practically necessary and at the same time objectively possible?' (Habermas, 1974, p 44) In Habermas' model of reflective practice, theory, research and practice are enmeshed or conjoined.

In this perspective, teaching is research and research is practice. Habermas adopts the existentialist assumption in Aristotle's philosophy, which is that teaching, like ethics and politics are not rigorous sciences but practical arts (Carr and Kemmis, 1986). In the Aristotelian conception of the practical arts, knowledge is uncertain and incomplete, theory is based in reflection and the concrete evidence of praxis leads to phronesis; a prudent and ethical understanding of what should be done in practical situations. In this sense, the critical theory position activates and is grounded in the interpretive categories of teachers, which is partly revealed in the evidence of their knowing-in-action: how they do their work and how they understand their doing at the stage of reflection-on-action.

But the critical theory position is not entirely subjective. It also acknowledges objective realities, or phenomena, that shape educational practices and can distort the subjective interpretations that teachers make. Horkheimer used the Marxian term 'false consciousness' to describe the effects of processes of socialisation into the objective reality of schooling, which can suppress and repress a subjective understanding of practice (Horkheimer, 1972). In other words, the critical theory position effectively problematises Shon's concept of knowing-in-action, on the basis that this practical process may tell us more about how effectively a teacher has been socialised and institutionalised into accepting, and therefore practicing, particular dominant values and pedagogical and epistemological selections, rather than providing an insight into how the emancipated, or fully conscious, practitioner might work if they were free to determine their own practice. It also destabilises the limits of knowing-in-action to include the influence of non-school knowing on practice knowing which is shaped by the existential experiences and objective realities of culture and social history. This is the basis of the emancipatory interest of critical theory: to reveal to us the extent to which our practices have been shaped by the objective realities of schooling systems and institutions which accept and reproduce social inequalities and to propose practical ways in which we can use this understanding to address the practical problems of how best to educate for a more ethical and equitable society.

> the task is to restore to consciousness those suppressed, repressed and submerged determinants of unfree behaviour with a view to their dissolution. (Habermas, 1974, pp 194-5)

There is, in this view, a dialectical relationship between a teacher's subjective practice or knowing-in-action and the objective reality of the school. The teacher's practice can shape the objective reality of the school but the school also shapes the teacher, and in so doing may repress the ethics, the desire and the aspiration of the teacher. Deborah Britzman has studied this dialectical relationship between individual teacher experiences and the shaping influence of their own educational histories and situations. Through critical ethnographic and narrative research she pieces together the ways in which teachers' knowing-in-action both shapes and is shaped by the objective realities in which they are socialised by educational institutions and their dominant ideologies (Britzman, 1991).

Critical theorists ask not only what knowledge is important in the curriculum but also whose knowledge, and what and whose interests such knowledge serves and how curriculum and pedagogy serve or do not serve different interests. Other feminist and post-colonial researchers and theorists working in the critical theory tradition have also revealed the hegemonic effects on the consciousness of teachers working within normative and naturalised school systems and institutions which deny, marginalise, or even violate the lived experiences of women, black minority ethnic communities, and other under-recognised voices (Grumet, 1988; Lather, 1991; hooks, 1998; Delpit, 1995; Giroux, 1996).

For me the highlight, Jon, was again the 3rd day. I really learnt something about myself as a teacher in the final scene...Because very briefly, two years ago, I found myself in a situation where a student presented a good, well written play about a controversial subject and the administration made it clear that this was not going on. And rather than fighting that, I acquiesced to that and found another place in the community where that could be produced and I felt I lost a lot of respect from the students for not standing up... Miss Screen, the dance teacher, found herself in a similar dilemma – she had a dance piece that dealt with a controversial subject that she wanted to present and administration said don't present it and she went ahead and she presented it in every concert and went out of teaching and is no longer teaching. What I found in the drama is that there are shades of grey. The fact that when you work under restrictions, not necessarily oppression, there is not just the case of being the hero and the case of being the coward and the complicitor but there are those shades of grey in the middle where you can work within the system. You can still remain in your teaching position and yet find ways of getting those messages to the students that they need to hear.

JN: How can we remain in our teaching positions and yet find ways of getting those messages to the students that they need to hear? How can drama be used as a critical tool in institutions that normalise the inequalities of power and inequities of social justice suffered by their inmates? What are my own personal boundaries in terms of how far I am prepared to go to challenge the dominant institutional messages? Is drama education necessarily political? If so, whose politics should be heard?

The structuring of experience and the process of enlightenment

Bourdieu suggests the concepts of 'habitus' and 'field' as dynamic tools for describing the dialectic between subjective and objective realities of schooling (Bourdieu, 1977). For Bourdieu, schooling is a structured structure, but it is also a structuring structure. It is both shaped by and in turn shapes the consciousness of subjects or agents. Deborah Britzman uses the formulation of 'the structure of experience and the experience of structure' to make a similar point (1991, p 28). In Bourdieu's theory there is a complex inter-relationship between the subjective concept of habitus which refers to the socially constructed habits and habits of mind, or the tacit knowledge to use Polanyi's term which guides the thoughts, feelings and actions of individuals and the objective structure or field in which habitus operates. Class, upbringing, cultural milieu and heritage shape a teacher's instincts and the teacher operates within the field of education, which is both structured by habitus and also structuring, or shaping, of habitus. From this perspective, knowing-in-action is the embodiment of certain social cultural messages, which have been learnt and internalised through various forms of socialisation. At its simplest, exploring this dynamic relationship between subjective experience and objective structures is akin to asking who am I and what do I do, and what does what I do tell me about who I am, and how I am being shaped by what I do and how, in turn, am I shaping what I do.

> The notion of habitus... is relational in that it designates a mediation between objective structures and practices... Social reality exists, so to speak, twice, in things and in minds, in fields and in habitus, outside and inside agents. And when habitus encounters a social world of which it is the product, it finds itself as a fish in water, it does not feel the weight of the water and takes the world around itself for granted. (Bourdieu, 1989, cited in Grenfell and Jones, 1998, p 14)

The two methodological tools of Habermas' critical science are ideology critique and critical action-research and Habermas proposed a four stage methodological model for creating an emancipatory praxis (Carr and Kemmis, 1986).

1. A description and interpretation of an existing situation that seeks to achieve what Weber described as Verstehen or a fuller understanding or *Gestalt*. Maxine Greene describes this process

as 'thinking big' about educational problems and contexts. Thinking big, she says, 'brings us in close contact with details and particularities that cannot be reduced to statistics or even to the measurable' (Greene, 1995, p 10).

2. An interrogation or 'penetration' of the reasons that brought the existing situation into being, which is close to the Frierian concept of *conscientisation* or the development of a critical self-consciousness, that seeks out and reveals the socio-historical and ideological dimensions of our conditioning. In order to act on and change the problematic situations in which we find ourselves, we first of all need to analyse how these situations have been socially and historically shaped and in whose interests (Freire, 1970, 1998).

3. Proposing an action-orientated agenda for altering or democratising the existing agenda (praxis).

4. Evaluation of the transformative and emancipatory effectiveness of the actions taken to alter the existing situation.

It is possible to identify this basic structure in more recent formulations of action-research, which tend towards a cyclical pattern of clarification, planning, action, reflection leading to further clarification and so on. The cyclical metaphor reinforces the on-going and unfinished task of reflective practice. In her summary of critical action-research, Zuber-Skerritt (1996, p 84) identifies a common sequence in models of action research, which she describes as:

1. strategic planning

2. implementing the plan (action)

3. observation, evaluation and self-evaluation

4. critical and self-critical reflections on 1-3 and making decisions for the next cycle of research

The ideas of reflective practice and the reflective practitioner, based on the common action-research cycle, have become commonplace in the normative and nomothetic discourses of education. Government documents and the aims of both initial and in-service training routinely refer to them as desirable characteristics for teaching. In England, formal and technical evaluations, or reflections-on-action, of teaching episodes are introduced in initial training and often become a required check on teaching performance in schools. The commodification of the reflective practitioner by policy makers and other powerful stakeholders in education has tended to mask the essentially radical and socially transformative roots of the concept.

I thought that Day 3 for me was the most engaged day for myself. I wished I had taken notes that day because afterwards I recalled all these different things. But I felt I was much more into the story of Pedro and I was very moved by what I was doing and what I was seeing... I mean I was ... I was like tears in my eyes at the end because I felt I was part of that story. I wish I could be more specific and I need to get notes.

JN: How can emotional engagement and identification become critical engagement leading to ideology critique of the situation? How do teachers balance the heat of emotional intensity with the need for cool reflection and intellectual intensity? What kinds of sympathy and empathy do I promote/develop in my work? Sympathy that is not also action, corrodes. (Edward Bond)

Critical and technical models of reflective practice

A distinction needs to be made, therefore, between technical and critical models of the reflective practitioner and reflective practice based on the application of the action-research cycle. The technical model is, as Elliot suggests, often limited to short-term inquiry and functional outcomes (1991, p 55). It tends also to limit the field of reference to controllable local instances rather than to the bigger socio-political context of schooling. Its aim is to fix localised problems, without necessarily identifying and acting on the apparently uncontrollable objective realities of the power structures that have shaped or conserved problems experienced at a local level.

There is a degree of idealism implicit in the critical theory research position, which is based on the assumption that teachers can take any kind of control over their working lives and practices when they are working within a highly legislated and prescriptive field, which is policed by inspectorates protecting the technical interests of government. Cohen *et al* question whether giving teachers as action-researchers a small degree of power to research their own situations in terms of 'habitus' and 'field' has any effect on the real locus of power and decision making which lies outside of their control (2001, p 32).

In the technical model of action-research one response can be to try and limit both the scope of the problem and the range of remedial action to the controllable. This often means creating manageable boundaries, both in terms of the scale and time period of the inquiry. This means that a teacher might go through an action-research cycle in order to evaluate whether, in the short term, a plan to improve her effectiveness in delivering an imposed scheme of work or curriculum objective such as the use of a prescribed course book or syllabus has an effect on her pupils' learning. The inquiry does not include a critical scrutiny of the scheme or objective itself, which may well be the cause of the local problems, such as where the imposed teaching is culturally or socially exclusive or where it inevitably favours certain groups of pupils rather than others. This level of analysis is seen as being outside the teacher's control and therefore unchangeable. The extent to which a teacher's knowing-in-action, in such a case, is limited and shaped by the external locus of power, which prescribed the curriculum, is not problematised, rather it is naturalised and considered as an immutable reality.

> When bonding happened we took it upon ourselves to bond.
>
> **JN**: How can the qualities of solidarity and comradeship associated with the ensemble be used to develop transformative and efficacious artistic/critical work?

This may only occur where action-research becomes separated from the radical and emancipatory desires implicit in the reflective practitioner position. It is a denial of hope in the sense that it suggests that the teacher abandons her belief in the possibility of change in the bigger world that surrounds the classroom. Critical theory emerges from the emancipatory struggles of marginalised individuals and groups; it belongs as Fanon suggests to the tradition of the oppressed. In this tradition, hope and the idea that the world is unfinished and capable of transformation become the basis for critical inquiry and emancipatory action in the face of seemingly impenetrable patterns of power and domination. Eagleton, puts this endeavour in these words:

One of the most moving narratives of modern history is the story of how men and women languishing under various forms of oppression came to acquire, often at great personal cost, the sort of technical knowledge necessary for them to understand their own condition more deeply, and so to acquire some of the theoretical armoury essential to change it. (Eagleton, 1996, p 53)

In adopting the critical reflective practitioner model in my practice as a drama educator I work in the expectation that change is possible, both in the locality of my teaching and also in the wider world beyond. I am particularly hopeful when I find myself working collaboratively with other teachers who are struggling to understand how to make their own teaching more equitable and critical.

The first day the work around Antigone was really interesting and by the end of that first day I had a really clear image of this young girl, this very little girl, really standing up to all this authority and I just found that really powerful... and as a father of a daughter it just struck a cord in me. When they are starting to be, you know, silenced it shows that girls about that age they are ahead of boys and everything and then all of a sudden there is this drop particularly in science and maths.

JN: What are the constraints on, and opportunities for, the public expression of personal responses to drama, leading to debate and potential social action? How can my work become more effective in eliciting these kinds of responses and the debate that can follow?

From common sense to ethical theorising

Because the reflective practitioner model describes an action-orientated and critically reflective and reflexive mode of praxis, rather than an orthodox or closed set of methods and procedures, it is not possible or desirable to try and categorise certain research methods rather than others. The other chapters in this book provide insights into different theoretical perspectives and research methodologies, which are inclusive of the reflective practitioner position and available for use in an action research-cycle. A reflective practitioner might use an eclectic mix of quantitative and qualitative methods and materials in order to help clarify, plan, implement and review progress in relation to praxis. In common with Brecht's critical dramaturgy, the reflective practitioner will make use of whatever means are ethically appropriate and technically necessary.

However, there are certain important characteristics which shape the selection of methods used in critical action research. These are concerned with perception, pragmatics and the role of common sense.

Critical action research is not empirical research. It is not based on auto-interpretations of observed phenomena. In critical theory there is the assumption that what we see, is what *we* see. In other words the same events and phenomena can and are experienced/observed/ interpreted differently by different people. The purpose of critical action research is to try and establish shared understandings or truth-claims. These shared understandings are negotiated through dialogue with others. The social and dialogic process of establishing the truth in critical action research is akin to Hannah Arendt's model of active citizenship in a shared space of appearances, in which she suggests that:

> Everything that appears can be seen and heard by everybody and has the widest possible publicity. For us, appearance – something that is seen and heard by others as well as ourselves – constitutes reality. Compared with the reality which comes from being seen and heard, even the greatest forces of intimate life – the passions of the heart, the thoughts of the mind, the delights of the senses – lead an uncertain and shadowy kind of existence unless and until they are transformed, deprivatised and deindividualised, as it were, into a shape to fit them for public appearance....The presence of others who see what we see and hear what we hear assures us of the reality of the world and of ourselves. (1958, p 50)

In this sense, the data and the interpretation of data must be problematised, so that they can be seen from other angles, rather than just from the perspective of the individual reflective practitioner. The problem identified by the practitioner may not in fact be the real problem. The interpretation may not be the interpretation, the proposed action may not be the right action. Truth has to be negotiated and based on different perspectives.

In a sense, critical action research attempts to bridge and exchange Grand Theory with local knowledge (Inglis, 1993). The local circumstances of the research site are mediated and illuminated through the lens of critical theory and critical theory is tested against the local circumstances of the problem under scrutiny. In critical action research we expect there to be some foundation of theory as well as the detailed investigation of the local context and its dynamics. However, teachers as reflective practitioners may need, for practical reasons, to find themselves a possible and manageable position on a formal-informal research continuum. The formal end characterises research done for academic purposes and audiences. This work is likely to be highly detailed and rigorous in terms of methods and truth claims. It will probably be closely referenced to methodological and critical theory. The informal end characterises work done for and with local colleagues with the practical purpose of suggesting ethical actions that might be taken in response to a locally identified and defined problem. This work will be representative of those involved and will be presented multi-vocally but it might not be as detailed and as closely referenced as an academic piece of work.

A third characteristic of critical action research methodology is the centrality of common sense as the bedrock for classroom inquiry. Rather than requiring teachers to learn new social science methods for research, critical action research is a process that begins with the everyday experiences, insights and knowing-in-action of teachers which is then theorised through self-criticism, ideology critique and the evidence gathered and analysed during the action research cycle. Gramsci described this process as a movement towards a 'philosophy of praxis' (1976, p 330) and Britzman suggests that in critical action research:

> The act of theorizing is not an imposition of abstract theories upon vacuous conditions. Theorising is a form of engagement with and intervention in the world. Theory always lives in the practical experiences of us all and yet must be interpreted as a source of intervention. (1991, p55)

I just wanted to pick up on that... I am tired of looking at teachers and dissecting them. I am so happy to sit here and just do it and be a part of it. You know people are coming up to me and asking what I felt about something you had done, and I said, 'yes, well I was engaged. I was just doing it. I am ready to go.' You just take me I am ready to go. I mean I was so happy doing it. Now what I do need to do is to go back and start to dissect, at least look at what was actually going on, but it was great. It's been a while since I have been able to do anything like this, years.

Jon, I would add to that it has been great to look at it as a teacher afterwards, but in the moment I was looking at it very much as a student and thinking this is what I need as a participant and this is the kind of thing that makes sense and how can we put this together?

JN: How can we negotiate a common truth for what we may see, hear and experience differently in drama? How can this best be done between internal and external agents such as audience/observers and internal agents and actors/leaders in a critical research context? How can this be done when there are unequal power relations?

Critical action-research may follow a process that is akin to Friere's descriptions of methodological rigour and research (Freire, 1998). Freire suggests that this process is a movement from ingenuous curiosity to epistemological curiosity. A movement from common sense curiosity about teaching and learning activity based on local knowledge, or 'folk knowledge' to use Bruner's term, towards an informed and critical hermeneutic based on the analysis of evidence which is multivocal and representative of the partnership of voices in the classroom and wider environment.

> It is my conviction that the difference and the distance between ingenuity and critical thinking, between knowledge resulting from pure experience and that resulting from rigorous methodological procedures, do not constitute a rupture but rather a further stage in the knowing process. This further stage... happens when ingenuous curiosity... becomes capable of self-criticism. In criticizing itself, ingenuous curiosity becomes epistemological curiosity, as through methodological exactitude it appropriates the object of its knowing. (Friere, 1998, p 37)

In conclusion, I tentatively suggest what I take to be certain characteristics of the kind of 'methodological rigour' that Friere describes, which for me describe also the lived values of a Reflective Practitioner.

Cyclical – reflective practice is an on-going commitment to ethical and committed teaching and learning and this is reflected in the cyclical and action-orientated model of action-research in which each cycle of identifying, planning, acting and reviewing creates the practical and theoretical impetus for the next cycle

Critical – reflective practice proceeds from the premises that the selection of knowledge is neither neutral nor natural and that unless we critique our own practices and common sense understandings of teaching and learning we are likely to normalise and naturalise the patterns of power and domination served by the selection process.

Emancipatory – critical reflective practice is intended to redress the imbalances of power and access to opportunity, which are embedded in normative and nomothetic curriculum selection, pedagogy and assessment. Through creating a radical praxis based on research, including self-criticism and ideology critique, teaching is seen as one important way in which we can intervene in the world and act for a more equitable and democratic society.

Evidence-based – at every stage of the action-research cycle the reflective practitioner gathers material and theoretical evidence which is used to clarify, interrogate, analyse, evaluate and inform the hunches, instincts and local knowledge which constitute a teacher's knowing-in-action. There is also a commitment to ensuring that alongside other forms of technical and material evidence there is also experiential and negotiated and iterated evidence which is representative of the partnership of voices in the classroom, particularly student voices, parents and other colleagues.

Ethical – As Britzman suggests, the existential and often contradictory experiences of living with the tension between a teacher's own ethical stance and the objective realities of schooling are at the heart of critical reflective practice. Reflective practice is a way of making some sense of these contradictions and for planning, proposing and implementing a praxis that strives towards a more inclusive and equitable, and therefore ethical, model of schooling.

Collaborative – Reflective practice pre-supposes a collaborative or collegiate approach to change which involves reflective practitioners working together to change their practices through discussion, shared action and evaluation. Taking collective rather than individual action is seen as a more effective form of intervention.

Reflexive – critical reflective practice seeks to model its social democratic values in the classroom, so that learning and teaching are based on open dialogue, negotiation and the fostering of critical thinking and action amongst the community of learners and teachers who have recognised and vocalised rights and responsibilities.

Note

1 These 'insertions' in the text are taken from a two hour semi-structured interview with the workshop participants held after the last workshop session. They are used here to interrupt the text with the voices of those taking part in the workshop.

JN marks my own problem-posing questions which are partly formed from my reflections on the interview and the issues raised and also on my observations and the video archive, notes, formal and informal discussions with both the observers and the participants and my use of an independent 'critical friend' who I trusted to give me unbiased feedback on my performance and to check out my own perceptions of the experience.

I realise now, as I reflect on the voices of the group and my own questions in response, that the central research theme is to do with issues of power and authority between the observers and the audience and the group and the teacher, and between the observers and the teacher. What I have begun to understand through my own reflective practice is that the epistemological and ontological differences between the researchers and the subjects in terms of what was experienced, understood, recorded and validated is highly problematic. What the reflective process suggests is that there needs to be a more open forum for the negotiation of the findings of the research – between researchers but critically between researchers and their subjects. The products of research must wrestle and fairly represent the feelings of disempowerment, silencing and appropriation voiced by the subjects at the close of the project (Ed).

Reference

Arendt, H. (1958) *The Human Condition*, Chicago, University of Chicago Press

Aoki, T. (1996)

Bernstein, J. M. (1995) *Recovering Ethical Life*, London, Routledge

Bourdieu, P. (1974) 'Schooling as a Conservative Force' in Eggleston, J. (Ed.) (1974) *Contemporary Research in the Sociology of Education*, London, Routledge

Bourdieu, P. (1977) *Outline of a Theory of Practice*, Cambridge, CUP

Bourdieu, P. (1989) 'Social Space and Symbolic Power', in *Sociological Theory* 7, pp 14-45

Britzman, D. (1991) *Practice Makes Practice*, Albany NY, SUNY Press

Carr, W and Kemmis, S. (1986) *Becoming Critical*, London, Routledge Falmer

Cohen, L, Manion, L. and Morrison, K. (2001) *Research Methods in Education*, 5th Edition, London, Routledge Falmer

Delpit, L. (1995) *Other People's Children: Cultural Conflict in the Classroom*, New York, The New Press

Dewey, J. (1933). *How We Think: A restatement of the relation of reflective thinking to the educative process*, Boston, DC Heath and Company

Eagleton, T. (1996) *The Illusions of Post-modernism*, London, Blackwell

Eggleston, J. (Ed.) (1974) *Contemporary Research in the Sociology of Education*, London, Routledge

Elliot, J. (1991) *Action Research for Educational Change*, Buckingham, OUP

Fanon, F. (1968) *The Wretched of the Earth* New York, Grove Press

Freire, P. (1970) *Pedagogy of the Oppressed*, Harmondsworth, Penguin

Freire, P. (1998) *Pedagogy of Freedom*, London, Bowmann and Littlefield

Gramsci, A. (1976) *Selections from the Prison Notebooks*, New York, International Publishers

Giroux, H. (1996) *Fugitive Cultures*, New York, Routledge

Greene, M. (1995) *Releasing the Imagination*, New York, Jossey-Bass

Grenfell, M and James, D. (1998) *Bourdieu and Education*, London, Falmer

Grumet, M. (1988) *Bitter Milk: Women and Teaching*, Amherst University of Massachusetts Press

Habermas, J. (1972) *Knowledge and Human Interests*, London, Heinemann

Habermas, J. (1979) *Communication and the Evolution of Society*, London, Heinemann

Habermas, J. (1974) *Theory and Practice*, London, Heinemann

hooks, b. (1998) *Teaching to Transgress*, New York, Routledge

Horkheimer, M. (1972) *Critical Theory; Selected Essays*, New York, Herder and Herder

Inglis, F. (1993) *Cultural Studies*, Oxford, Blackwell

Kinchloe, J. (1991) *Teachers as Researchers*, London, Falmer

Lather, P. (1991) *Getting Smart: Feminist Research and Pedagogy with/in the Post-modern*, London, Routledge

O'Neill, C. (1995) *Drama Worlds*, Portsmouth, NH, Heinemann

O'Toole, J. (1992) *The Process of Drama*, London, Routledge

Shon, D. (1987) *Educating the Reflective Practitioner*, San Francisco, Jossey Bass

Taylor, P. (2000) *The Drama Classroom: Action, Reflection, Transformation*, London, Routledge Falmer

Zuber-Skerrit, O. (1996) *New Directions in Action Research*, London, Falmer

Reflective Practitioner and Critical Action Research Methodologies:

Altrichter, H. Posch, P and Somekh, B. *Teachers Investigate their Work*, London, Routledge

Cohen, L, Manion, L. and Morrison, K. (1993) *Research Methods in Education 5th Edition*, London, Routledge Falmer (Chapter 13 – Action Research)

Carspecken, P. (1996) *Critical Ethnography in Educational Research*, New York, Routledge

McNiff, J (2002) *Action Research Principles and Practice – 2nd Edition*, London, Routledge

McNiff, J. Lomax, P. and Whitehead, J. (2003) *You and Your Action Research Project – 2nd Edition*, London, Roultledge Falmer

Silverman, D. (2000) *Doing Qualitative Research*, London, Sage Publications

Reflective Practice:

Berry, K. (2000) *The Dramatic Arts and Cultural Studies,* New York, Falmer Press

Britzman, D. (1991) *Practice Makes Practice*, Albany, NY, SUNY Press

Carr, W and Kemmis, S. (1986) *Becoming Critical*, London, Routledge Falmer

Gallagher, K. (2000) *Drama and Education in the Lives of Girls Toronto*, UTP

Greene, M. (1995) *Releasing the Imagination*, New York, Jossey-Bass

Heathcote, D. (1982) 'Signs and Portents?' in Neelands, J. and Dobson, W. (eds.) (2000) *Theatre Directions*, London, Hodder and Stoughton

Kinchloe, J. (1991) *Teachers as Researchers*, London, Falmer

Lather, P. (1991) *Getting Smart: Feminist Research and Pedagogy With/In the Postmodern*. New York, Routledge

Norriss, J. McCammon, L and Miller, C. (2000) *Learning to Teach Drama; A Case Narrative Approach*, Portsmouth, N.H, Heinemann

Taylor, P. (2000) *The Drama Classroom: Action, Reflection, Transformation*, London, Routledge Falmer

Zuber-Skerrit, O. (1996) *New Directions in Action Research*, London, Falmer

3

Researching Through Case Study

Joe Winston

If a painting by Magritte confirms one's lived experiences to date, it has, by his standards, failed; if it temporarily destroys the experience, it has succeeded. (Berger, cited in Simons, 1996, p 233)

The search for certainty, comparison and conclusiveness tends to drive out alternative ways of seeing. (Simons, *ibid*, p 237)

What is case study?

Case study is a methodology, a way of approaching educational research, that has proven to be both flexible and popular among teachers and student teachers, particularly those interested in researching into their own practice. As Hammersley and Gomm point out, case study as a concept is not limited to research contexts (2000, p1). Lawyers, medical practitioners, social workers and detectives all study cases as part of their work. As a form of educational research, it maintains a connection with this kind of inquiry in its concentration upon the single case. Its intention is to further our understanding by concentrating on depth rather than breadth. In the words of Robert Stake:

> Case study is the study of the particularity and complexity of a single case, coming to understand its activity within important circumstances. (1995, p xi)

Can Focus More

However, despite its intrinsic pragmatism, it would be misleading to approach case study solely as a methodology, as the quotations that introduce this chapter hint. Its emergence in the 1960s and 1970s as a form of educational inquiry had both epistemological and political significance. It afforded a kind of knowledge and a way of knowing that supplemented, and indeed challenged, dominant forms of research, piloting a democratisation of the research process in educational contexts.

One of the first advocates of case study for the purposes of educational research was Lawrence Stenhouse. Stenhouse was the leading figure in the 1970s among those encouraging teachers in the UK to become researchers into their own practice. He explained the purpose of educational research as an applied rather than a pure form of inquiry. Research, he proposed, should first and foremost be useful, serving the purpose of educational improvement, of bettering practice through enhanced understanding. To this end, he saw teachers as the best researchers of practice, operating in localised research communities. His vision of teachers as extended rather than restricted professionals became the engine of the movement towards action research that grew in the 1970s and 1980s.

Simons (*ibid* 1996, pp 228-231) presents a synopsis of case study history since its growth in the 1970s that explains the epistemological revolution it initially promised. The late 1960s and early 1970s were a time of great optimism and educational innovation. However, traditional models of evaluating innovations, following a positivist paradigm, modelled upon an objectives model of curriculum planning, lacked the flexibility to judge the complexity of the range of new programmes being trialed. In her words:

> It became important to study the innovation in context to try and understand the broad range of factors that contributed to the success or failure of the innovation; to capture the complexity of the interactions as the innovative ideas were interpreted in practice; and to understand the uniqueness of the case. (*ibid* p 229)

The political nature of evaluation, Simons explains, led case studies to become qualitative rather than quantitative in nature, providing space for the perceptions of the participants and seeking ways to convey a valid sense of the experience of a programme as well as its effects. One of the key evaluatory possibilities of case study inquiry is to inform the judgment of policy makers. If more traditional models of evaluation strove to provide conclusions and closure, the strength of case study was to do the opposite. It offered policy makers opportunities 'to reconstruct their own understanding in order to inform their judgment ... it rendered policy making uncertain .. the unfamiliar familiar and the familiar strange' (*ibid* p 230).

As Simons wryly points out, this type of case study is not always perceived as a strength by policy makers, especially in the current educational climate. Consequently, case study research has in many quarters lost its sense of radical epistemological challenge. In response to the requirements of sponsors and the nature of research contracts, case study design, flexible as it is, has tended in recent years to become trimmed to respond to the 'pressure for certainty' (*ibid* p 231). But I would argue that it is in the epistemological and political principles and opportunities that characterised its rise to prominence that drama educators can find a form of research that not only can respond to their practical needs but, perhaps more significantly, can chime with the forms of knowledge generated by the art form of drama itself.

A key tension at the heart of case study is the relationship between the uniqueness of its terms of reference and the generalisability of its results. The subjects of case studies can be various: a child, a class of children, a school; a lesson, a scheme of work; a teacher, a department. But if we accept Stenhouse's concise definition of research as 'systematic inquiry made public' (1980, p 1) what kind of knowledge the making public can generate is a question in need of careful consideration. The increased understanding generated by the inquiry may be of interest to those in the research frame but may not be of value to those in the broader educational community?

Stake's response to this question at the heart of case study theory is to define the generalisations emanating from case study research as naturalistic. These he distinguishes from the propositional generalisations sought for in scientific inquiry.

> Naturalistic generalisations are conclusions arrived at through personal engagement in life's affairs *or by vicarious experience so well constructed that the person feels as if it happened to themselves.* (1995, p 85, my italics)

This form of knowledge has long been associated with the learning one acquires from narrative fictional art forms, drama included. To seek to reduce all valid knowledge to the measurable and the scientifically proven may fit with the logical positivism that currently dominates political discourse on education but it is epistemologically unsound. Case study research contributes to knowledge in the way Bruner defined narrative'as opposed to paradigmatic'forms of knowing. If the latter strive for universal truths dependent upon logic and proof, the former gain their weight from verisimilitude, dealing as they do with the vicissitudes of human intention (1986, p 16) Although case study theorists have argued with Stake, questioning the sufficiency of his definition, they tend not to quarrel with the thrust of this perspective on the kind of knowledge generated by case study. Donmoyer (2000), for example, in basing his own understanding of case study generalisation upon Piaget's schema theory, still stresses the essentially artistic nature of case study research and the reader's response to it. Interestingly, he uses the following personal story to illustrate his point.

> When I was in my early teens, I had an opportunity to see Arthur Miller's *Death of a Salesman*. Though the Willy Loman on stage and the adolescent who sat in the darkened theatre had little in common, I learned a great deal about myself that night. Despite the many differences between Miller's ageing salesman and the adolescent who watched him – or possibly because of these differences – something, which in ordinary parlance could be called generalisation, occurred. (*ibid* p 55)

The real power of case study to generate new knowledge can be likened to the knowledge generated by the best forms of drama. As the quotations opening this chapter suggest, it can challenge and disrupt our common sense understandings; it can help us see problems where we had not seen them before, question what had hitherto remained unquestioned, understand a familiar experience viewed from other perspectives.

Such an argument in favour of the significance and appropriateness of case study research for the drama practitioner has implications for how we approach it, in particular for the kind of knowledge we seek to gain when embarking upon it. Simons' advice to the researcher includes the following principles:

- challenge existing forms of knowing through using different ways of seeing

- approximate the way of the artist .. in aspiring to describe and interpret those encounters

- embrace the paradoxes inherent in the people, events and sites we study and explore rather than try to resolve the tensions embedded in them (Simons, *ibid* p 237)

In addition I would propose that we use case study to seek out rather than solve problems, provoke rather than answer questions, deepen our understanding rather than rush to closure. In fact as any good drama would be used.

Some methodological considerations

See all factors

The case study method allows investigators to retain the holistic and meaningful characteristics of real life events. (Yin, 2003, p 2)

Given this central aim of case study practice, methodological approaches, varied and flexible as they may be, nonetheless present researchers with a considerable challenge. When designing our methodology, as Simons reminds us, we would do well to return to the concept of artistry. Just as we choose from the conventions available to us when creating a piece of theatre or planning a drama lesson, so too with research methods. We craft our methodology to pursue our aims, evaluating and re-evaluating it, adapting and refining as we proceed. The focus of our attention may shift or may progressively narrow as we journey through the research event; a revised methodology may be called for as we perceive new questions arising or as we recognise the inadequacy of our design. Just as the creative act of devising theatre can take the participants through the highs and lows of discovery and despair, so too the emotional journey of the researcher can be rocky and uncertain. It is part of the course and not a sign of failure.

As with any research design, issues of ethics and validity are of central concern to case study. Ethical questions relate to the public nature of research and need to be negotiated in relation not only to its human subjects but also to the meanings that researchers construct from their findings and argue in their reports. Ethical issues are not always easily separable from those related to the validity of the research and they impinge on the process from its inception.

45

Whether we can legitimately gain access to necessary information, how we intend to conduct our observations and interviews, how we choose to share our interpretations with subjects before publication: all these are ethical issues to negotiate at the moment of design and to review as the research progresses.

Arguments over case study validity tend to relate to issues of sub-jectivity as much as they do to the generalisability of findings. Such arguments revolve around questions discussed above and concern the nature of knowledge itself. As Robinson points out, however, the distinction between subjectivity and objectivity is not as clear as is always argued (2001, pp 70-74). Objective knowledge in science is knowledge that a group of experts in the field, having studied and observed, agree to be valid. For this reason, it was a scientific fact for centuries that the sun orbited the earth. It took a paradigm shift in scientific understanding before a new scientific fact could be agreed upon. So although scientific laws are 'discovered knowledge' rather than 'constructed knowledge' (Stake, 1995, pp 99-102), objective knowledge of this kind is nonetheless dependent upon inter-subjective agreement among experts in the field.

> Science strives to build universal understanding. The understanding reached by each individual will of course be to some degree unique, but much will be held in common. Although the reality we seek is of our own making, it is a collective making. We seek the well-tuned reality, one bearing up under scrutiny and challenge. (Stake, 1995, p101)

In this way case study researchers seek validity both in the research process and in the way they present their findings. The concept of *triangulation*, of actively seeking perspectives other than one's own, is the common approach but it will only work if the researcher is open and responsive to judgments different from her own and refuses to prioritise those that support what she already thinks. This is as much an ethical issue as it is one of validity and is recognised as such by Stake:

> It is true that in case study we deal with many complex phenomena and issues for which no consensus can be found as to what really exists – yet we have ethical obligations to minimise misrepresentation and misunderstanding. (1995, p 108)

He usefully provides us with four categories of triangulation:

- *Data source triangulation*, where we attempt to see if what we are observing and reporting carries the same meanings when found under different circumstances (p 113)

- *Investigator triangulation*, where we invite other investigators to look at the same scene from their particular perspectives

- *Theory triangulation*. This approach is intimately related to investigator triangulation and actively seeks out different theories to explain what is happening in the research event

- *Methodological triangulation*, where we design multiple approaches into our methodology. Interviews with participants, consulting relevant documentation, member checking, all are meant to ensure that any interpretation is supported and qualified by a range of data

One drawback with the concept of triangulation is the mathematical nature of its metaphor. It implies that a single perspective is what we seek, one correct interpretation. This may not be the case. Rather than always attempting to confirm a single meaning, we may feel it appropriate to document alternative understandings of the same event. This ethnographic approach to research introduces us to Geertz's concept of *thick description* or setting down the meaning particular social actions have for the actors whose actions they are (1993, p 27). If we accept that all social knowledge is constructed, that meaning is necessarily interpretative, the tensions between description and explanation, observation and interpretation are at the heart of the meaning making process in any research event. The case study approach is a suitable methodology for forefronting this awareness.

Approaches to case study research in action

The subject matter of the world in which the educational researcher is interested is ... subjectively structured, possessing particular meanings for its inhabitants. The task of the educational investigator is very often to explain the means by which an orderly social world is established and maintained in terms of its shared meanings. (Cohen and Manion, 1980, p 103)

In her opening address to the conference Gallagher introduced us to the notion that, as researchers, we should regard observation as context rather than judgement. But what kind of observers were we at the research event of IDIERI 2003? Yin distinguishes between 'direct observation' and 'participant observation' (2003, pp 92-93). Cohen and Manion argue that, given the nature of the educational researcher's task, participant observation has four inherent advantages (1980, pp 103-104):

- It allows for non-verbal as well as verbal data to be gathered

- It allows the investigator to make appropriate notes about ongoing behaviour as it emerges

- It enables the researcher to develop a more intimate and informal relationship with those he is observing

- It is flexible and less reactive to more structured data gathering methods, where unnoticed bias can remain unaddressed through the very rigidity of the research design

We could debate the degree to which those of us who were observing the drama sessions at IDIERI were participants or not but the four advantages listed above were available to us as researchers over the week. In particular, if we consider the event in its uniqueness, as a performance as well as an educational event, with researchers as audience and students and teacher as actors, then we can argue that researchers were *participants in* the event as well as *observers of* the event. It is precisely this uniqueness of the experience, in fact, that became the focus of inquiry for one of the groups established in our research station.

In our first group session, I proposed that we organise the week's sessions in such a way as to journey through the research process together, using our time to theorise the practice of research rather than the drama practice we were witness to. Once this was agreed, each of the sessions could be planned to cover the different phases of the research process, namely:

- Finding a research focus and defining a researchable question

- Planning a suitable methodology

- Gathering, collating and analysing data

- Preparing to report on our findings

The intention was for us to find research questions that genuinely interested us and to allow for as many research groups to emerge as was necessary to investigate our points of interest. In brainstorming after the first session, we were able to group these interests into four areas. One concerned the nature of drama as pedagogy, another the nature of the learning, a third the aesthetics of space in this particular drama event and a fourth the complex nature of the event itself from the perspective of the participant observers. Our need now was to re-fine these into four researchable questions.

Yin's approach to case study is a pragmatic one, defining it as the most apt research strategy to answer how and why questions, espe-cially when researchers have little or no control over the events under study. This he defines as an *explanatory* purpose but he also pro-poses two further purposes for case study research, *exploratory* and *descriptive* (2003, Chapter 1) Bringing Yin's categorisation to bear on the questions that emerged, I originally classified them as follows in Figure1:

Figire: 1	
Purpose of case study	**Example of research question**
Explanatory	What are the students' perceptions of this particular learning experience? How does the teacher use questioning when attempting to deepen the students' learning?
Exploratory	What is the nature of this master class as a performance event?
Descriptive	How were the malleable aspects of the space managed by the teacher and to what effect?

With only minimal interrogation, however, in the true spirit of the conference title, these categorisations look artificially imposed and begin to collapse. As with much case study theory, they are useful to provoke reflection – in this example, they help us consider the thrust of each inquiry – but all three case studies had integral elements of the explanatory, the exploratory and the descriptive.

I chose Stake's work as the theoretical reading for our station, given its clarity of style, precision of argument and its explicit vision of case study research as an art. We considered his ideas for a given section of each session, not to accept blindly his categorisations but to use them as a springboard for theoretical reflection. Two sets of distinctions he proposes were of immediate use as we considered the kind of questions that might provide focus for our varied research interests. First of all, he distinguishes between the *intrinsic case study* and the *instrumental case study* (Stake, 1995, pp 3-4). With the former, it is the particularity or intrinsic nature of one particular case we are interested in, whereas with the latter we are interested in gaining insights of a more generalised nature, in using the case as an instrument to look at broader issues. We did not regard these binaries as fixed but used them as analytical frames around which to theorise our practice as researchers. At the outset my thoughts were that those in the groups involved in the explanatory case studies were driven by instrumental concerns, that those in the descriptive study were embarking on an intrinsic case study, whereas those in the exploratory group were engaged in an inquiry of equally intrinsic and instrumental interest.

The other of Stake's categories we considered at the outset was the distinction he proposes between *etic* and *emic* issues. Etic issues are those questions that we consider before embarking on the research, questions we consider of interest because of existing theory, previous research or our own informed experience. Emic issues are those that emerge from within, during the research process itself. If etic issues are a necessary part of our planning, emic issues are an inevitable outcome of reflection throughout the research process. The two sets of issues will therefore tend to exist in a dialogical relationship, the one encouraging us to reflect upon and reconsider the other. However, with instrumental case studies, etic issues are likely to be pre-eminent, as emic issues are in intrinsic case studies.

One agreement we reached very early on was ethically motivated. Jonothan Neelands had volunteered to have his practice scrutinised over a period of days. We were not here to admire but to inquire. Any praise of his practice that emerged from our research would of necessity be made public, as is the nature of research, but so would any critique. As there was no way in which the identity of this particular teacher could be protected, we agreed to focus our varied inquiries, whatever they might turn out to be, away from anything that might smack of evaluation or judgment of the practitioner.

So were we conducting four separate case studies into the one event? Yin makes an interesting distinction between 'holistic' and 'embedded' case studies (p 42-45). In a holistic design is used for examining the global nature of a programme whereas an embedded design concentrates on different subunits to focus attention more precisely. If holistic designs tend to be conducted at an abstract level, with little attention to specific measures of data, embedded designs help focus an inquiry but sometimes fail to attend to the larger unit of analysis. In this case, our subunits of analysis were meant to be distinctive and were not chosen to provide a comprehensive study into the entire drama event. They were therefore four distinct studies rather than four embedded units in one holistic inquiry.

I now look at how two of these studies progressed, having chosen the two with the more unusual foci of inquiry to concentrate upon. In each example, I will to present the case from the researchers' perspectives before making comments of my own. These are not intended to be evaluatory in any way but to expand upon the methodological considerations that each provokes. Any good case study needs to establish its contextual references clearly. These group members lead busy professional lives and travel to conferences not only to learn but also to re-establish professional contacts and to enjoy the social aspects of the gathering. Any inquiry they engaged in was limited in terms of both time and energy and would necessarily culminate more as work in progress than as a finished piece of work.

Sample case studies 1: use of space

A trio of teacher leaders from Australia, the UK and the US chose to embark on an inquiry into the teacher's use of space. Their initial researchable question was 'How were the malleable aspects of the space managed by the teacher and to what effect?'. This led them into other areas of associated interest, significantly an investigation into the pattern of power within the space. For this purpose, they drew up an observation sheet that they completed themselves during each of the subsequent sessions. They also asked student participants and observing researchers to complete their own sheets at the end of each session. An example is provided as Appendix 1 (p 62).

As the week progressed, the group became interested in the way that thematic concepts of the drama, as well as its aesthetic elements, could be spatialised. The circular nature of the theatre space used for the teaching led them to explore these concepts in the form of a

51

series of concentric circles which they presented to the conference in their report. See Figures. 2, 3 and 4.

Figure 2

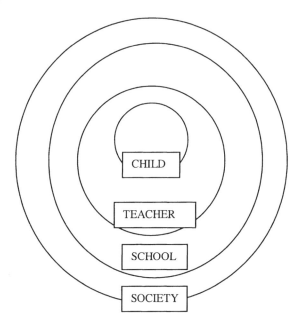

Figure 3

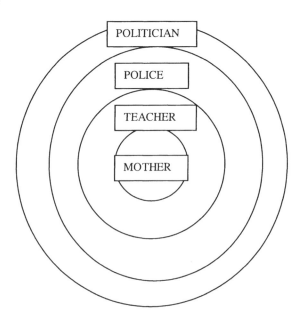

Figure 4

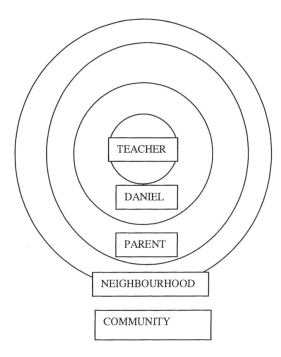

This is how one member of the group described their experience in an email several months later:

> My notes identify a number of areas where we thought there were parallels between the space and the thematic concerns of the workshops. We looked at this with a model of concentric circles – from the core of the workshop group, to the outer circle of the audience, to the boundaries of the hall and beyond to any audience outside. Thematically, this was reflected in the consistent local-global progressions Jonothan was using: for example: child- teacher-school-society on 15th July, or mother-teacher- police-politician on 18th July and finally on the same day – tramp-Daniel-parents-neighbours. This was connected to power and the identification of a particular hot-spot which Jonothan used a number of times but this began to recede as the week progressed.

From this exercise they framed a second researchable question: 'How was the metaphor of concentric circles realised spatially and thematically in the work?'

Considerations for developing such a project
I initially saw this study as descriptive but in the final analysis it was far more exploratory in nature, offering the possibility of further

questions and approaches to research in this area. As with the work of all the groups in this station, I was fascinated by the theoretical possibilities opened up and with the methodological challenges afforded to further research.

The observation sheets provided a large amount of stimulating detail, as the example in Appendix 1 illustrates. In examining these sheets the recurring pattern of circles first became evident to the group. So the process of recording three-dimensional space in a two dimensional form was successful in leading to new perceptions when the data was revisited. A larger study might wish to consider the following issues to make collation of evidence both easier identification of emergent themes:

- Asking the observer to mark their own position in to the space

- Piloting the sheet, both by researchers and participants in drama lessons, and acting on feedback to make recording of data more focused and retrievable

- Finding a way of involving all respondents who used the observation sheets to reflect upon thematic as well as organisational/aesthetic/power-related issues as they related to the use of space

- Possible ways of including more ethnographic evidence, capturing more sustained accounts of what it was like to be in different parts of the space at key moments in the drama

- Different critical lenses through which to view the space, in both physical and thematic terms, such as from the perspectives of race, class and gender

- Due consideration of theory. This would need to be extensive and include theories on spatial semiotics and in how dramatic meaning can be influenced by the location of actors in space (e.g. Alfreds, 1980), how power is expressed theatrically in social space (e.g. Geertz, 1980) and how concepts can be interpreted and classified through spatial analogy and metaphor (eg Deleuze and Guattari, 1987)

- The use of video as a key element of the research methodology.

This last point is particularly important as videoed evidence would provide a durable record to permit further viewings of the drama work and would enable a scrutiny of complex spatial signifiers beyond the scope of an observation sheet. If we take the issue of power, for example, then the vertical as well as horizontal patterning of space is significant, as are the dynamics of various participants' movements through it and various groups' occupation of it at key moments. For example the research station that looked into feminist approaches scrutinised videoed evidence to see if there were any noticeable differences between male and female use of space.

Sample case study 2: master class as performance

The group that inquired into the master class as a performance event was composed of four experienced practitioner-researchers from four different countries. The transcript of the group's own résumé of their inquiry handed to me on the final day of the conference, precedes my own commentary.

Figure: 5
The master class as performance: a case study by four researchers as participants? observers? audience? students?

Research question: what is the nature of the master class as a performance event?

Definitions – master class – other terms – we eventually felt that we liked term master class but included the others as those points of view were important, too. So we honoured many voices but represented primarily our own four-person point of view.

Performance. That definition was important in relationship to theatre.

Data gathering. We relied primarily on our notes. We observed different things and sometimes the same things. Our debriefings between the days often influenced what we looked for on the next day. Sometimes information we learned between sessions or during sessions also became sources of data. Sometimes we asked people questions but the primary sources of data were our fieldnotes.

Data reduction. In our last discussion after the final session we agreed that the focus of our case would be on our responses or, more importantly, our questions about this event. Recognising that we represent a certain level of experience as teacher-leaders but different cultural traditions (US, Israel, Australia, New Zealand) – we felt we could 'see' difference/sameness.

1. We wrote questions we had from our experiences, separately. When we compared our lists we found points of overlap.

2. Our lists were collapsed to one list, including just those items we all agreed to.

> **Figure: 5 (continued)**
> **The master class as performance: a case study by four researchers as participants? observers? audience? students?**
>
> 3.   From the master list we created categories and these became our four major findings.
>
> 4.   Each item from our master list was assigned to a category.
>
> *Presentation of the report.* Starting with the conference theme, we set our destabilising questions in the context of the conference brochure.
>
> Just about everything in our presentation was framed as a question. We had no answers, only questions from our experiences.
>
> As a coda: we found we learned from each other and very much enjoyed our reflections together.

The group decided to perform their report, speaking questions individually, signalling different levels of puzzlement and engagement through gesture, tone of voice and facial expression. Examples of the questions scripted under their four headings are presented below.

Nature of the event
- Who performs? What do they perform and to whom?

- What is a participant?

- What resemblance does a master class have to a drama education experience?

Learning
- What is the value of being a participant?

- Who changed? Who learned?

- What kind of knowledge do we extract from a master class?

Power
- Who has power? Who has control? How does the nature of the master class dictate or influence this?

- I can't hear. Am I supposed to hear?

- This is our space!

Personal

- When was I engaged? When shut out?

- There are circles within circles. Where am I at this moment?

- Could I ever put myself out there?

Considerations for developing such a project

The group knew quickly what they wished to focus on but spent some time debating issues of language, interpretation and definition before agreeing on their research question. So the choice of the terms master class and performance was the result of careful deliberation, clearly signalling how the very language we use as researchers can pose problems for us as it inevitably carries metaphorical inference and ideological weight. We may be bounded by language but we need to remember that it is laden with values and is seldom a conveyor of simple, transparent meanings. Their care with language is also playfully initiated as they destabilise the categorical terms open to them to define their roles as researchers within the context of this research event.

The methodology was limited to the field notes of the group members, which also included informal recordings of other delegates' perspectives. It is evident from their comments that this process was dynamic throughout. The broad parameters of their research question became refined and more narrowly focused as they shared their developing impressions from session to session. This approach exemplifies Stake's advice that we should not separate issues of data analysis and interpretation from data collection. 'Analysis is a matter of giving meaning to first impressions as well as to final compilations (p 71)'. Given that the research question does not limit itself to their own perspectives, a more complete study would either redefine the question to signal this limit or actively seek to include a broad range of perspectives. These could have included other researchers, students, Neelands himself, those members of the conference who had prior experience of working as master teachers, conference organisers and those research station leaders from outside the drama education tradition. This would necessarily preclude a broader methodology, including questionnaires and interviews with focus groups and individuals.

Interestingly, although the group's data gathering was limited to field notes, the term they use for collation and analysis is data reduction. This again accords well with Stake's advice, offered in the form of a quotation from Wolcott:

> The critical task in qualitative research is not to accumulate all the data you can, but to 'can' (i.e. get rid of) most of the data you accumulate. This requires constant winnowing. The trick is to discover essences and then to reveal those essences with sufficient context, yet not become mired trying to include everything that might possibly be described. (Stake, 1995, p 84)

In searching for meaning, we tend to scrutinise our data for pattern and repeatability. Yet the single, disruptive instance that creates a moment of aporia can often be just as illuminating. The group's account of their process of collation demonstrates a systematic approach to a search for emergent themes and provides us with a good example of how inter-subjective meanings can be constructed in an open, democratic fashion, ensuring that no one perspective dominates the process.

Perhaps the most interesting reflections that this group's approach provokes is in their report, in both the form and content. It immediately signals the significance of audience. A conventional research report would follow the outline in Figure 6 (opposite), which I have used to assist Masters students with the structure of their dissertations. Stake argues that if a report's main job is to assist in the validation of naturalistic generalisation, communication with a reader is essential and a clear description of context important.

> To develop vicarious experience for the reader, to give them a sense of being there, the physical situation should be well described. (Stake, 1995, p 63)

The audience for this report had quite literally *been there* so the usual conventional parameters were already irrelevant. Instead, there was an opportunity to experiment. There is no doubt that the nature of their inquiry embraced the epistemological case for case study presented earlier. Their purpose was to problematise, to make strange, to seek further questions rather than provide answers. Hence the report of their findings exactly reflects the spirit of their inquiry.

Figure: 6

Conventional model for a research report

Introduction.
State clearly the focus of your inquiry. Why was it chosen? Why was it significant enough to research? What is your stake in it? Who might be interested in your report and why?

Review of the Literature.
Engage with the on-going conversation of your educational community. What has been written about this area? What theories have been put forward? What relevant research has been carried out and what has it proposed?

Context.
Where and when did you research? Who were your subjects? Why them? What shape did this research take? Any constraints, opportunities, particular difficulties that made you change your plans at any point?

Research methodology.
Any particular paradigm that influenced your research design (eg action research/ethnographic approaches/reflective practitioner)? What data gathering methods did you employ and for what specific purposes? What were your specific practical and ethical considerations? Did you then run into any specific problems, practical or ethical, that made you refine or revise your methodology? How did you collate and analyse your data?

Analysis.
The bulk, the main course, the substance of your report. Key themes emerging from your analysis could be discussed under subheadings. Carefully relate theory to practice by reference to other texts. Argue, do not advocate. Be critically attentive to detail. Do not be frightened of uncertainty. Be modest and speculative but robust in your argument.

Conclusion.
So what? For you/your site of practice/your colleagues/your students/for the wider educational community of which you are a part?

Appendices.
Relevant documentary evidence. Sample questionnaires. Statistical breakdown. Contextualising of quotes taken from evidence (journal/video/audio recordings) that you have included in your main text. Photos.

Thoughts for your case studies

With any research question it is useful to consider who cares? before embarking upon it. Similarly, when considering the findings of a research report we should ask ourselves: so what? Such a report will be of little use unless it has some influence on future action. The second group's coda testifies to the learning they gained from the experience of researching together but what about a broader public?

Largely due to changes in funding policy within higher education institutions, there has been a marked growth internationally in educational research over recent years and the master class has been piloted at previous IDIERI conferences as a possible means of exploring a range of significant issues at the interface between theory and practice. This study is the first I have come across where a group of drama specialists have attempted to inquire into it rather than simply comment upon it. In limiting their findings to a series of questions, they are suggesting a possible agenda for future conference leaders to address if they want to engage with the problematic elements of power and performance that impinge upon the development of knowledge that the master class should provoke.

Recommended Reading

Cohen L. and Manion L. (1980) *Research Methods in Education*, London, Croom Helm

Chapter 5 of this book is devoted to Case Study. The authors provide illustrated examples of systematic approaches to participant observation studies, concentrating their attention on methods of data gathering rather than data analysis.

Geertz, C. (1993) *Thick Description: Towards an Interpretive Theory of Culture in The Interpretation of Cultures*, London, Fontana

A seminal text, in which Geertz argues the implications for social and anthropological research of a semiotic approach to cultural inquiry. He stresses the importance of understanding context if we are to offer interpretations of what people are doing and why. He likens the job of the case study researcher to that of the literary critic and sees the value of single case studies in the theoretical perspectives they afford others who will study similar social processes in different cultural settings.

Golby M. (1997) *Case Study as Educational Research*, University of Exeter (ISBN 85068-141-3)

A short, concise and illuminating overview for the beginner.

Gomm R, Hammersley M. and Foster P. (2000) *Case Study Method*, London, Sage

A collection of theoretical commentaries organised into two sections entitled Intrinsic Case Study and Gereralizability and Case Study and Theory. Contributions by Lincoln and Guba, Donmoyer and Becker (Chapters 2, 3 and 11) are particularly useful.

Simons H. (1996) The Paradox of Case Study in *Cambridge Journal of Education*, 26(2)

An essential article for drama specialists embarking upon case study research, one that I have drawn upon extensively in this chapter.

Stake R. *The Art of Case Study Research*, 1995, London, Sage

A key text, highly accessible, coherent and easy to read. Stake's approach to case study design and epistemology should strike chords with drama educators.

Stenhouse L. (1978) Case study and case records: towards a contemporary history of education, *British Educational Research Journal*, 4(2)

Stenhouse draws parallels between case study inquiry and the work of historians, arguing that in both cases knowledge is verified through communal criticism of evidence and is intended to map the range of experience rather than discover predictive scientific laws. Such generalisations he defines as retrospective rather than predictive.

Yin R. *Case Study Research: Design and Methods*, 2003, London, Sage

Essential reading for the PhD student using case study methodology. Yin's pragmatic stance embraces qualitative and quantitative methods. His detailed analysis of the processes of applied research is thorough and analytical but well illustrated and accessible.

Additional Bibliography

Alfreds M. (1980) *A Shared Experience: the Actor as Storyteller in Theatre Papers: the third series*, Dartington, UK

Bruner J. (1986) *Actual Minds, Possible Worlds*, Cambridge Mass, Harvard University Press

Deleuze G. and Guattari F. (1987) *A Thousand Plateaus*, Minneapolis, University of Minnesota Press

Donmoyer R. (2000) Generalizability and the Single-Case Study in Gomm R. *et al Case Study Method*, London, Sage

Robinson K. (2001) *Out of Our Minds*, Oxford UK, Capstone

Stenhouse L. (1980) The Study of Samples and the Study of Cases in *British Educational Research Journal*, 6(1)

Appendix 1

PARTICIPANT/OBSERVER   Date *18ᵗʰ July*

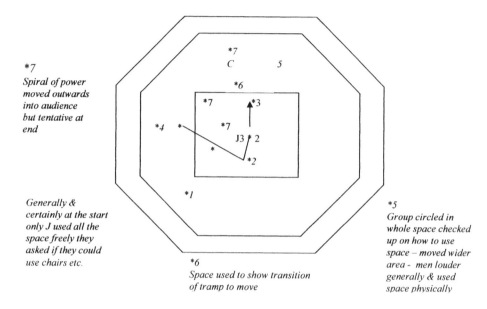

*7
*Spiral of power
moved outwards
into audience
but tentative at
end*

*Generally &
certainly at the start
only J used all the
space freely they
asked if they could
use chairs etc.*

*5
*Group circled in
whole space checked
up on how to use
space – moved wider
area - men louder
generally & used
space physically*

*6
*Space used to show transition
of tramp to move*

*1 one group consistently uses the space front left of the mats – students generally stayed on or just off
mat*

2 J's progress while looking at images – often eyes look at him looking at images

*3 student politically insistent got sidetracked into exercises – power temporarily came from opposite J
difficult to ignore – managed it!*

*4 baseball game – in audience student took power by use of 'audience' back & addressing audience –
fronting them.*

We are interested in the relationship between space and power. Think about how space was managed in today's workshop.

What were significant moments for you in the workshop and where were the participants in the space? (mark on the map)

Where was Jonothan (mark him separately) and what do you think he was aiming to do?

4

(Post)Critical Ethnography in Drama Research

Kathleen Gallagher

C ritical ethnography, marking an important evolutionary moment within the field of educational ethnography, provokes an apt research modality for examining the social and artistic relationships and performances inspired by drama work. The critical nature of critical ethnography, as it has come to be termed, is profoundly interested in the relationships of power reproduced in spaces, marked by differently positioned subjectivities. A critical epistemology for drama research is especially fitting because the activity of drama itself is about taking up positions and spaces to examine the worlds they produce. If drama is indeed a man in a mess, as celebrated drama pioneer Dorothy Heathcote once proclaimed, then critical ethnography becomes one fascinating way to deconstruct and understand how it all came to be. The dramatic world has infinite stories to tell the actual world; it is both informed by it and fleeing from it. In return, critical ethnography offers the dramatic world rich theoretical scaffolding in order to help the researcher interrogate both the situatedness and the agency of the drama's and the classroom's characters.

The classic, realist ethnographic text has been productively revisited in this post-modern moment. Critical ethnographic inquiry of drama observes the phenomena that allow people to function in a particular drama education classroom culture while taking account of the researcher's impact on the context under study. The ethnographer's gender/race – neutral self within a realist story about the other (Spivak, 1990; Trinh, 1989) opens onto the multiple truths and discourses that operate in a social and aesthetic space. Some ethnographers (see Ball, 1990, p 43) have attempted to systematise the ways in which the critical ethnographer can remain self-reflective in her/his processes by urging the researcher to become a 'reflexive analyst.' This would involve a continuous weighing of the impact of their presence and the participants' perceptions of them against the usefulness and limitations of the data recorded. These self-reflexive processes also help to keep researchers vigilant about the ways in which their research methods might be implicated in the reproduction of systems of oppression. According to critical epistemology, the subtleties, and sometimes invisibility of oppression must be challenged. Lather's (1986) notion of 'face validity,' discussed later, becomes important as a means by which the interpretations made by researchers are examined and recognised as credible by the research participants themselves.

Critical ethnographers in drama research engage in questions of interpretation and representation of both the social reality and the drama practices in an education setting. Critical refers to the substantive theoretical frames, such as feminist, neo-Marxist, and/or Freirian emancipatory, shaping the study and ethnography refers to the qualitative methodology and its ensuing paradigms and assumptions.[1] Unlike other interpretivist ethnographic research, critical ethnography's goal is to expose and even challenge unequal power relations by examining the dialectical relationship between social/structural constraints on human actors[2] and the possibilities of human agency. It is what Lather (1986) has termed 'openly ideological research'. Theoretical frames of gender, sexuality, class, and race inform critical ethnographic studies in the field of education because of a general dissatisfaction with research accounts of structures such as class, patriarchy, racism, heterosexism, in which actors do not appear and a dissatisfaction with accounts of actors and cultures in which these structures do not appear.[3]

So critical ethnographic research asks:

- how we represent

- how we evaluate the legitimacy of our representations and

- whether it is possible to effect change in the world

To this important set of research and pedagogical interests I would also ask of critical ethnographic research in drama classrooms, the extent to which research of dramatic worlds and relationships can offer a special leverage on our understanding of actual worlds and relationships suggest different possibilities or actions that might help us redress issues of social justice more broadly. In other words, I suggest that through studying how drama teachers and participants work in role with each other and through theatre genres, the non-linear and narrative modes of drama education can productively interrupt our traditional qualitative accounts of classrooms and theatre studios and the people who enliven them. The new ethnography, as Denzin (1997) describes it, has crossed that liminal space that separates the scholarly text from its subjects; we are all co-performers in our own and others' stories. Denzin's use of theatre/performance metaphors is not accidental if we are all both the stars of our own performances and the secondary characters in a range of developing plots which surround us.

How critical ethnographers of drama classrooms might differ from more mainstream ethnographers is in their belief that qualitative analytic categories for drama such as 'archetype,' 'metaphor,' 'belief in role,' 'consensus and collaboration,' 'gender-roles,' 'character' and other grand narratives of drama research are not simply helpful concepts for describing what goes on in drama classrooms but are part of a process which can reproduce a particular set of social relationships. Critical drama ethnographers would resist seeing the above categories as purely descriptive and nonproblematic. They would insist that language is central to the formation of subjectivity and that certain narratives (archetypal, metaphoric, etc.) are privileged over others. As Anderson (1989, p 254) has pointed out, for critical ethnographers the ideological nature of knowledge resides in the embeddedness of commonsense knowledge and social science knowledge in political and economic interests. For critical ethnographers a reading against recognition and identification, a reading that challenges a self-evident present, interrupts conventional analytic categories and incites other ways to construct and read ethnographic narratives. Both dramatic and ethnographic trans-cendence are thus confronted.

Eisner and Peshkin (1990) talk about locating our cognitive maps to help us find our way in the territories we wish to explore and that those with different maps, like case study or narrative methodologies, tend to take different roads. Critical ethnography predisposes the researcher toward holding the tension between the conditions of a territory that enable/constrain human actors *and* the actions of actors that might break through the limiting aspects of circumstance. Critical feminist theorists since the 1980s began to focus upon the interpenetration, as Dilorio (1982) called it, of structure and con-sciousness in the situations and relationships of everyday life. This structural/individual 'interpenetration' of critical research therefore coheres with drama's pedagogical preoccupation with the relation-ship between self and the world, the individual and the group, the self in relation to others.

On the question of validity, some have made the accusation that far too much legitimising of critical ethnographic studies has reverted to positivist and even quantitative measurements. Lather (1986) has helpfully taken to task systems of knowledge production that answer to questions of validity without examining the ways in which parti-cipants' involvement in such research promotes self-understanding and self-determination, or what she has termed 'catalytic validity.' This idea of explicitly designing research for the contribution in may add to the self-defined emancipatory goals of a group is central to critical ethnography's project. Lather and others have also cautioned that these rigorous, self-conscious, and reflexive processes must also keep the critical framework from becoming a mere container into which the data is poured; it must not be theory-dense at the expense of its transformative potential. Ultimately, the conversation between critical social theory and ethnographic methods must retain its pro-ductive dialectical tension. To do so involves a special commitment to praxis, that is that ethnographers assume that both theory and prac-tice must speak to each other and are equally present in any given moment, embedded within one another. Adkins and Gunzenhauser (1999) go further still and suggest that '... the value of knowledge is rooted in their conversation rather than in either individual construct' (p 67).

Critical ethnographers at work in Northampton 2003

In the research station titled Critical Ethnography, researchers spent a good deal of preparatory time thinking about the 'picture of our looking.' As researchers interested in emancipatory agendas and the contribution our research might make toward that goal, we began 'from ourselves,' as Dorothy Smith's (1987) feminist methodology would encourage. We began, then, with an attempt at beginning to uncover our assumptions about observing a group engaged in drama by considering Deborah Britzman's article 'The Question of Belief: Writing Poststructural Ethnography' (2000). In this article, Britzman (citing Rooney, 1989, p 37) asks the reader to take Althusser's opposition to textual innocence seriously: 'There is no such thing as an innocent reading, we must ask what reading we are guilty of.'

The questions, therefore, that emerged for us from Britzman's work asked:

- ▨ what is it that structures my own stories and my own intelligibility?

- ▨ what do my moral imperatives cost?

- ▨ how do I read the absent against the present?

- ▨ if critical ethnography is always about a 'second glance,' what might my second glance be wanting to discover?

Reading the absent against the present, according to Britzman, is the way in which post-structuralists disturb the promise of representation in ethnographic interpretation:

> Thus, the ethnographic promise of a holistic account is betrayed by the slippage born from the particularity of language of what cannot be said precisely because of what is said, and of the impossible difference within what is said, what is intended, what is signified, what is repressed, what is taken, and what remains. (2000, p 28)

Leaving behind a sentimental ethnography that desires to represent without looking back, she explains, means discovering what our second glance might imagine. What might be possible in ethnography's second glance and, 'is there a knowledge ethnography cannot tolerate knowing?' asks Britzman. These were among the most important questions asked before even considering our move into the field. Not to do so would be to assume a kind of theoretical naiveté. Of course, as a diverse group of researchers, we are bringing a range of implicit assumptions to our 'observation' tasks. Attempts to identify some of these assumptions, our governing interpretations, the frames and positions and readings enabled by this diverse group, became a necessary starting point.

Because conducting educational research is both about studying and creating culture, as critical researchers we began on the first day with some particular questions about the kind of culture we were poised to encounter. First, keeping alive the tension between our use of critical theory and our deployment of ethnographic methods like participant observation and interviewing, we began by asking what happened in our observation of the drama on day one that made concrete the various critical theoretical frameworks we were discussing. In other words, we were interested, first, in asking how culture is contested terrain rather than a set of shared patterns (Quantz, 1992). Reading Quantz (1992) and Britzman helped us to grapple with questions of power as central to the social encounter we were observing and in which we were participating. Quantz deploys a Foucauldian framework for encountering notions of power through critical ethnographic work in the study of everyday life. Foucault (1990) wrote:

> Power's condition of possibility... must not be found in the primary existence of a central point, in a unique source of sovereignty from which secondary and descendant forms would emanate; it is the moving substrate of force relations which, by virtue of their in-equality, constantly engender states of power, but the latter are always local and unstable. The omnipresence of power: not because it has the privilege of consolidating everything under its invincible unity, but because it is produced from one moment to the next, at every point, or rather in every relation from one point to another. Power is everywhere: not because it embraces everything , but because it comes from everywhere... One needs to be nominalistic, no doubt: power is not an institution, and not a structure; neither is it a certain strength we are endowed with; it is the name that one attri-butes to a complex strategical situation in a particular society. (1992, p 93, cited in Quantz)

In our case, we aimed to observe encounters of power relations in the everyday classroom life of drama participants. It is this theorisation of power as everywhere and produced from one moment to the next that we attempted to work with in the discussions following our observations. A second notion from Quantz' argument also remained central to our post-observation discussions. In this instance, Quantz is rooted in Habermas' notion of 'emancipatory interest.' The Habermasian argument suggests that efforts to limit historical-structural analyses, rather than being free of values, actually end up serving the interests of the ruling elite.

> Because values must always enter into research and because some interest is always being served by research, critical ethnographers opt for those values that promote transformation of oppressive societies toward emancipation and democracy. (Quantz, 1992, p 473)

So we set out in our fieldwork to determine what were the emancipatory interests in this particular context. What relationships might be served by a critical interrogation? Who is empowering whom? And finally, as all critical frameworks must ask, how do we see the concept of power and relationships of power as central to the social context of the drama workshop?

How do the dialectics of self and other, of local and global, of democracy and domination play out in drama's pedagogy?[5] How do the players and teacher come to understand the dialectical relationship between what we deem performative (role-playing) and what we often assume is non-performative (students in a classroom or workshop). There is an intertextual relationship between the fictional roles enacted in the dramas and the so-called real ones of classroom or workshop life. Given the additional conference expectation to construct our critical ethnographic narrative to share our findings on the final day of the conference, we asked how we might produce an ethnographic text as collage in the way that Clifford (1980), in his influential essay 'On Ethnographic Surrealism,' imagined:

> The cuts and sutures of the research process are left visible; there is no smoothing over or bending of the work's raw 'data' into a homogeneous representation...The ethnography as collage would leave manifest the constructivist procedures of ethnographic knowledge; it would be an assemblage containing voices other than the ethnographer's, as well as examples of 'found' evidence, data not fully integrated within the work's governing interpretation. (p 563-564)

Once in the field, theory *became* our analytic categories. I defined these as 'moments of rupture/rapture' because we were asking ourselves to enter into the aesthetics of the drama work and pedagogy (its rapture) by theoretically un/settling provisional meanings (the ruptures) and taking account of researcher positionality vis à vis our relative attraction to/distance from the work.

Different researchers bring different moments forward. With critical ethnography it is not a simple question of observing more, for the aim is not ultimately to capture a complete picture. Accepting that observation will always be partial and positioned, produced through interested discourses, we discussed a shift from the notion of observation as a method *per se* to a perspective that emphasises, as Angrosino and de Perez (2000, p 676) describe it, 'observation as a context for interaction among those involved in the research collaboration.' If, as critical researchers, we take this idea of observation seriously as context for interaction, we had to begin by speaking with participants themselves, to understand how best to get to the meaning structures given by the participants to explain their experiences. Quantz (1992) posits that 'culture should always be understood to refer to both the structured patterns of a group and the meanings members give to those patterns' (p 486). For example, prior to observation, each ethnographer approached a participant and asked of her/him the following: How can I best observe you/your work to gain the most insight?

After a second day of observation, a second ethnographic glance, and given the compressed nature of the research project, we began to contemplate how we might best interview some of the participants. True to a critical agenda, the interview schedule was a list of four questions, based on both the things that the research participants told us to observe and things we felt we were getting closer to wanting to pursue in our inquiry. Working in pairs, our group members collectively designed lists of four questions. This emergent design enabled us to identify the explicit desires of both the research participants and the researchers.

Once both field observation and interviews were carried out, the critical ethnographers moved into a mode of 'playing with data.' This 'playing' was the way of making concrete Van Maanen's (1988) call for 'impressionistic tales' in ethnography. Van Maanen explains that impressionistic ethnographic tales are characterised by:

...their silent disavowal of grand theorising, their radical grasping for the particular, eventful, contextual, and unusual... They attempt to be as hesitant and open to contingency and interpretation as the concrete social experiences upon which they are based. (p 119)

This was also how, methodologically and analytically, post-structuralism was useful. For instance, we consciously elucidated the intertextual features of our research site: the social and dramatic contexts. What questions, in the context of the drama world, were left unanswered by participants? And conversely, what observations of the cultural dynamics in the group penetrated the drama constructions/imaginaries? Context as observation, therefore, meant that the playful and serious mechanisms of Jonothan Neelands' drama structures and context would become part of our ethnographic tale and significantly inform our understanding of the 'real' social reality.

What features of Neeland's drama facilitation pressed back against our realities as drama practitioners and researchers? What features of the participants' created drama work pressed back against our observations of the social context? Jonothan Neelands' choice of texts and sources gave us much food for critical thought. In playing with the data, we produced a physical collage. The large picture Neelands used at the outset of one lesson, the image that asked his audience to decide which of the two figures was taller, became the backdrop against which we placed pieces of his source material. On top of this image of perspectivism, we placed the story of the teen jailed for killing a homeless man. Adhered to this story, we pasted the story of Pedro Malbran from Siria School, grade three: 'What My Family Does At Night.' This layering of imagined reality atop lived reality compelled the intertextual dialogue so crucial to research of drama education. Using an ethnographic imagination, we queried what these imagined stories might have to do with the material realities of the research participants. We were, therefore, asking what the pedagogic environment created by Neelands and the fictional school and society created in the dramas by the participants might have to say to our observation and interview data. Was there a dialectical relationship between the real and the fictive? If so, how would we know? What insights about our participants might help us evaluate the artistic work produced? What aspects of the drama might help us grasp other parts of our partial views of participants and the dynamics between them? In playing with the data, we ultimately constructed some collective images of our fieldnotes and interviews. In the interests of inter-textuality we brought these worlds into conversation, not because this would necessarily help us 'know the other' to any greater extent, but because this would give us insight into the culture we observed and were now attempting to reconstruct.

It seems to me that questions of validity are particularly important to articulate, for critical ethnographic epistemology sets itself apart from assumptions underlying traditional positivist conceptions of knowledge and inquiry. In our moments of validation of our know-ledge construction, Lather's (1986) validity categories, 'Face', 'Con-struct' and 'Catalytic', became especially useful. Face validity is Lather's term for a member-check and is operated by recycling data, observations, analyses, conclusions, back through at least a sub sample of participants. Construct validity aims to determine whether the actual constructs, are not mere inventions of the researcher's per-spective, but are occurring. And perhaps most importantly, as critical methodologists, we needed to check our meanings against parti-cipant meanings to discover the extent to which our findings might reveal the degree to which the research process re-orients, focuses, and energised participants in what Freire (1972) terms 'conscientiza-tion' (p 67). Hence, catalytic validity. To these important measure-ments of validity, more attuned to the critical epistemology and qualitative approach of the research, I have added two additional categories for critical ethnographic research of drama education. The first is Dramatic/Aesthetic Validity and the second Pedagogic Validity. Dramatic validity addresses the degree to which the drama work has shaped and been shaped by the social culture; pedagogic validity recounts the degree to which the drama facilitation and pedagogic choices have enabled artistic ownership and character/plot deter-mination. These two notions of validity are, of course, intimately con-nected.

Further possibilities for critical ethnographic studies of drama projects

One could imagine a wide variety of drama research contexts in which these five post-positivist narratives of research validity can be engaged, with some caveats for each. Face Validity, in Lather's terms, has to do with participants' own assessment of the research dis-coveries, hence, knowledge construction, rather than simply knowledge production. The challenge for critical ethnographers is how they set potential dissonances (from participants) up against their own provisional understandings, rather than subsume them into some authoritative research narrative; how, in short, the researcher makes decisions both in the field and in the writing to guard against the potential hegemony of her/his own critical interpretation. Construct validity, in its efforts to distinguish between real and contrived constructs may be understood to be favouring a certain kind of so-called objectivity neither possible nor desirable in poststructural analyses. Catalytic validity relates to Lather's concept of openly ideological research but it would be a mistake to assume that Lather is talking about biasing our research in ways that we deem ideologically correct. Rather, it is an attempt to hold critical ethnography accountable to its ideological foundations. In other words, our critical methods must not unwittingly be part of the reproduction of oppression and domination and should instead be part of movements toward social equality. Dramatic/Aesthetic validity is not about a valuation of the aesthetic qualities according to some set of aesthetic norms. On the contrary, the dramatic or aesthetic validity of a project will measure the degree to which perspectives in the dramatic world are informed by the breadth and variety of social actors contributing to the work. Finally, Pedagogic validity is not simply a measure of a drama teacher's skill even if there was consensus about what that is but a marker of the quality and depth of inclusion and discovery-based, open-ended or self-directed learning in which participants can engage.

As critical researchers, we began to bring these notions of validity to our data. Limited by time, I would suggest that the categories of validity I have put forward – both Lather's and my own – not act as a kind of checklist for research but inform the selection of methods, the kinds of interviews, the evaluation of the drama I have not included a particular measurement for the evaluation of the drama work itself, its artistic value. While proponents of the field of drama education often speak as though one immediately recognises and that there is universal agreement about what constitutes 'good work,' the goal of critical ethnographic work is different. Critical ethnographic research of drama classrooms is interested in questions of social justice, of inclusion and participation, of self- and other-understanding, of liberatory pedagogy. My assumption is that one consequence of liberatory pedagogy is good drama work. This conjecture is, obviously, contestable and my constructs of dramatic and pedagogic validity may be limited by such a supposition or that unequal power relations are bad, such as that equal power relations are attainable and good for the art. Nonetheless, I would still argue that a high degree of dramatic and pedagogic validity will improve both the quality of the experience for the social actors and their artistic outcomes.

Some limitations

Criticisms of critical epistemologies in research suggest that they are flawed by bias and the principles of reciprocity, even political correctness. The same criticisms might be levelled against liberatory practices in drama education, but I maintain belief that the possibilities for rich, imaginative and artistic work are increased by a group's investments in the variety of forms of participation and the equity-centred processes through which one's participation is enabled. Often, like good drama, critical ethnographic research takes time and can involve very lengthy discussions about the relationship between theory and data, the effects of the researcher's presence on the data which makes a virtue of specificity in ways that both enhance and restrain its impact and the imperfect capacity to measure effects. On this count, Adkins and Gunzenhauser (1999) caution that critical ethnography's 'retreat into the familiar theory corner' may result in impact that is merely 'a hope,' rather than a tangible means to ensure a percolation between the local site and the academy where ideas of transformation may reside. The 'marriage,' as Noblit (1999) calls it, of critical theory and ethnography, indeed blossomed in its early days, yet there are currently criticisms of the union that include a silencing of polyphony, male domination, and theoretical oversimplification of power relations. Noblit concludes that postcritical ethnography 'is not one thing, rather it is a critical space where many things can go on simultaneously' (p 4).

At IDIERI 2003, the research station titled Critical Ethnography became just such a space for engaging with the complexity of factors and relations of power at work. As researchers, we took on a macro-analysis of our research site, favouring large structural processes and insights. The microanalysis of other methods like narrative or case study are sometimes directed toward more personal rather than structural understanding or change. But critical ethnography might also be served by greater attention being paid to discourse analysis so that the relationship between linguistic and non-linguistic activity, in drama classrooms especially, might more systematically reveal how relations of power are sustained through the creation and reproduction of meaning. 'If you had a year,' I asked the researchers in the end, 'If you had a year... how would you structure your observations and interviews to gain the most insight about the artistic and social relations produced through the unique collaborations of drama work?'

A challenge

I close this chapter by offering three persuasive reasons why critical ethnography, and its 'posts,' is a particularly suitable research methodology and framework for studies of drama education. The first is a simple one: the critical tradition in education is always changing and evolving, constantly informed by new disciplinary practices. There is the opportunity to develop flexible research methods for the drama classroom that do not limit the creativity and trans-disciplinarity that so often energises it. Critical social research has not produced a tight methodological school of thought. Designs, field techniques, and interpretations have enjoyed a proliferation rather than a narrowing or refining of possibilities. Second, the tension of the individual and the group, the self and other dichotomy of drama worlds may help researchers pay exacting attention to the ever-present theoretical tension between structures and agency at the core of critical ethnographic epistemologies.

And finally, while Foucault (1980) reminds us of the disciplining nature of the social sciences more generally and the 'regimes of truth' that tell us who we are and what is or is not possible for us, the critical ethnographer of drama has the opportunity to bring the 'stories' of the 'marginalised other' to a critical agenda in order to examine the discourses and practices that maintain such inequalities. Grumet (1991) and others have continued to point to the power of narrative in curriculum. If drama, then, is powered by narrative and if these narratives, particularly of the 'outsider', are brought into productive dialogue with the critical traditions of emancipatory or democratic agendas in education, the drama classroom will have a powerful role to play in 'storytelling as a negotiation of power,' as Grumet portrays it.

Delgado (1989, cited in Pignatelli, 1998) talks about the significance of disenfranchised groups telling what he calls 'counter-stories.' In this telling, he argues, both outsider and listener gain:

> Oppressed groups have known instinctively that stories are an essential tool to their own (psychic) survival and liberation... Listening to the stories of outgroups can avoid intellectual apartheid. Shared words can banish sameness, stiffness, and monochromaticity and reduce the felt terror of otherness when hearing new voices for the first time. (pp 2436-2437, 2440)

Listening to and telling stories is the lifeblood of drama activity. Each individual within the group is engaged in a self-other dialogue; the group, too, is occupied with the always shadowy interplay between real and imagined worlds. This constant referential and reflexive space in drama education creates fertile ground for the dialectical tension at the heart of critical ethnographic research.

Fine (1994), however, is concerned with the potential for 'othering' in ethnographic research and argues, instead, for an attentiveness to 'working the hyphen,' between self (researcher) and other (research participants who necessarily have less [speaking] power). Simply doing drama is one way to extend the borders of who gets to tell which stories. In other words, drama is 'which man in whose mess?' Now we're talking! In essence, critical ethnography's persistent concern with the potential dangers of 'othering' is aligned with drama's post-modern, multi-perspectival narrative devices that have the potential to extend interpretive power, interrupt master narratives and deeply engage in the self/other dichotomy at the very core of any understanding of power relations and agendas of democratic and transformative pedagogies. And if, indeed as some are arguing, we find ourselves in a 'post-critical' ethnographic moment, our accounts of drama classrooms will need to move beyond mere description and ensuing theorisations of oppression toward a more reflexive dialogue about praxis. This might be achieved, in part, by relying more heavily on the checks and balances of pedagogic and dramatic validity. A post-critical ethnographic epistemology in drama research, with an emphasis on the pedagogical and dramatic *processes* at work in the research site, may indeed implore research participants both to participate in the knowledge construction of the research event and take real strides toward a lasting impact on the pedagogical and dramatic realms within which they will continue to live long after the research has ended.[4]

Notes

1   To be clear, 'critical' in this instance is not a negation of reality but an historically contextualising look at reality, the circumstances and relationships between people that are often taken as unexamined and de-historicised assumptions.

2   In this chapter, I shall refer to the participants of the research as 'actors.' When I am referring, by contrast, to dramatic actors, I shall do so explicitly.

3   See Anderson, Gary L. (1989) Critical Ethnography in Education: Origins, Current Status, and New Directions, *Review of Educational Research*, 59(3), 249-270 for an account of critical ethnography's dissatisfactions on the one hand with critical theory's excessively theory-driven accounts, and on the other hand, critical theory's dissatisfactions with ethnography's atheoretical and 'neutral' accounts. To this earlier argument, I have added heterosexism as a more recent concern of critical ethnography's explicit challenge to forms of domination and oppression.

4   See Gallagher, K. (in press) Theories of the Stage, Social Projects, and Drama's Pedagogies, *Applied Theatre Researcher/IDEA.*

Recommended Reading

Prerequisite Readings for IDIERI 2003

Britzman, D. (2002) 'The Question of Belief': Writing Poststructural Ethnography, in E. A. St. Pierre and W. S. Pillow (eds) *Working the Ruins: Feminist Poststructural Theory and Methods in Education*, New York, Routledge

Quantz, R. A. (1992) On Critical Ethnography (with Some Post-modern Considerations), in M. D. LeCompte, W. L. Millroy and J. Preissle (eds) *The Handbook of Qualitative Research in Education*, pp 447-505, New York, Academic Press

Book Chapters

Kincheloe, J. L. and McLaren, P. (2000) Rethinking Critical Theory and Qualitative Research, in N. K. Denzin and Y. S. Lincoln (eds) *Handbook of Qualitative Research*, second edition, pp 279-314, Thousand Oaks, CA, Sage

Books

Carspecken, P. F. (1996) *Critical Ethnography in Educational Research: A Theoretical and Practical Guide*, New York, Routledge

Dei, G. J. S., Mazzuca, J., McIsaac, E. and Zine, J. (1997) *Reconstructing 'Drop-out': A Critical Ethnography of the Dynamics of Black Students' Disengagement from School*, Toronto, University of Toronto Press

Denzin, N. K. (1997) *Interpretive Ethnography: Ethnographic Practices for the 21st Century*, Thousand Oaks, CA, Sage

Journal Articles (annotated. Abstracts adapted from ERIC Database)

Anderson, G. L. (1989) Critical Ethnography in Education: Origins, Current Status, and New Directions, *Review of Educational Research*, 59(3), pp 249-270

   Abstract: This review traces the development of critical ethnography in education, including a brief discussion of its view of validity; discusses its current status as a research genre; describes criticisms and suggests new directions

Jordan, S. and Yeomans, D. (1995) Critical Ethnography: Problems in Contemporary Theory and Practice, *British Journal of Sociology of Education*, 16(3), pp 389-408

Abstract: Asserts that ethnography's development out of anthropology left it tainted with biases from colonialism and imperialism. Discusses several contemporary approaches, including critical ethnography, really useful knowledge, and action research. Suggests further incorporation of post-modern ideas into the field of ethnography

Pignatelli, F. (1998) Critical Ethnography/poststructuralist Concerns: Foucault and the Play of Memory, *Interchange*, 29(4), pp 403-423

Abstract: Uses a post-structuralist and post-modernist critique, anchored in Foucault's work, to inform a critical ethnography, contending that one way to open up more room for critical and imaginative dialogue about fairness, decency, and respect is to encourage the play of memory in ethnographic text. The paper demonstrates the utility of memoirs as a useful narrative device within a critical research agenda

Adkins, A. and Gunzenhauser, M. G. (1999) Knowledge Construction in Critical Ethnography, *Educational Foundations*, 13(1), pp 61-76

Abstract: Explores the grounding of cultural critique in ethnography as a process of knowledge construction, using concepts from philosophy, anthropology, and sociology of knowledge to identify a theory of knowledge that may inform a post-critical ethnography. The paper proposes a critical ethnography that is more authentic both to its wider social project and its internal methods of practice

Tricoglus, G. (2001) Living the Theoretical Principles of 'Critical Ethnography' in Educational Research, *Educational Action Research*, 9(1), pp 135-148

Abstract: Discusses issues surrounding teacher research and the validity of qualitative study, exploring one teacher researcher's route through a small-scale qualitative study. The article uses attempts to implement a critically ethnographic approach and dilemmas of trying to live the theoretical principles of the research methodology as the basis for suggesting a theoretical framework for teacher research

Noblit, G. W. (1999) The Possibilities of Postcritical Ethnographies: An Introduction to This Issue, *Educational Foundations*, 13(1), pp 3-6

Abstract: This paper introduces a theme issue on ethnography and critical theory. The five articles within the issue provide an understanding of the space of post-critical ethnographies, each looking at the topic from a different viewpoint. Together, they reveal that the future marriage of critique and ethnography will be vibrant.

Warren, J. T. (2001) The Social Drama of a 'Rice Burner': A (Re)constitution of Whiteness, *Western Journal of Communication*, 65(2), pp 184-205

Abstract: Explores, through critical performance ethnography, the performative constitution of whiteness in an introductory communication classroom. Suggests that white subjects often fail to see whiteness in action. Argues that race in general, and whiteness in particular, is a social communicative accomplishment – a performative constitution of identity instituted and maintained by repetitions of meaningful acts.

References

Adkins, A. and M. G. Guzenhauser (1999) Knowledge Construction in Critical Ethnographic Foundations, *Educational Foundations*, 13(1), pp 61-76

Anderson, G. L. (1989) Critical Ethnography in Education: Origins, Current Status, and New Directions, *Review of Educational Research*, 59(3), pp 249-270

Angrosino, M. V. and de Perez, K. A. M. (2000) Rethinking Observation: From Method to Context, in N. K. Denzin and Y. S. Lincoln (eds) *Handbook of Qualitative Research, second edition*, pp 673-702, Thousand Oaks, CA, Sage

Ball, S. J. (1990) Self-doubt and Soft Data: Social and Technical Trajectories in Ethnographic Fieldwork, in M. Hammersley (ed) *Educational Research: Current Issues*, London, Paul Chapman

Britzman, D. P. (2000) 'The Question of Belief': Writing Poststructural Ethnography, in E. St. Pierre and W. Pillow (eds) *Working the Ruins: Feminist Poststructural Theory and Methods in Education*, pp 27-40, New York, Routledge

Clifford, J. (1980) On Ethnographic Surrealism, *Comparative Studies in Society and History*, 23, pp 539-564

Delgado, R. (1989) Storytelling for Oppositionists and Others: A Plea for Narrative, *Michigan Law Review*, 87, pp 2411-2441

Denzin, N. K. (1997) *Interpretive Ethnography: Ethnographic Practices for the 21st Century*, Thousand Oaks, CA, Sage

DiIorio, J. A. (1982) Nomad Vans and Lady Vanners: A Critical Feminist Analysis of a Van Club, Unpublished doctoral dissertation, The Ohio State University

Eisner, E. W. and Peshkin, A. (eds) (1990) *Qualitative Inquiry in Education: The Continuing Debate*, New York, Teachers College Press

Fine, M. (1994) Working the Hyphens: Reinventing Self and Other in Qualitative Research, in N. K. Denzin and Y. S. Lincoln (eds) *Handbook of Qualitative Research*, pp70-82, Thousand Oaks, CA: Sage

Foucault, M. (1980) *Power/knowledge: Selected Interviews and Other Writings, 1972-1977*, C. Gordon (ed), New York, Pantheon Books

Foucault, M. (1990) *The History of Sexuality, Volume I: An Introduction* (R. Hurley, Trans.), New York, Vintage

Freire, P. (1972) *Pedagogy of the Oppressed*, London, Penguin

Gallagher, K. (in press) *Theories of the Stage, Social Projects, and Drama's Pedagogies*, Applied Theatre Researcher/IDEA

Grumet, M. (1991) The Politics of Personal Knowledge, in C. Witherell and N. Noddings (eds) *Stories Lives Tell: Narrative and Dialogue in Education*, pp 67-77, New York, Teachers College Press

Lather, P. (1986) Research as Praxis, *Harvard Educational Review*, 56(3), 257-277.

Noblit, G. (1999) The Possibilities of Postcritical Ethnographies: An Introduction to This Issue, *Educational Foundations*, 13(1), pp 3-6

Pignatelli, F. (1998) Critical Ethnography/poststructuralist Concerns: Foucault and the Play of Memory, *Interchange*, 29(4), pp 403-423

Quantz, R. A. (1992) On Critical Ethnography (with Some Post-modern Considerations), in M. D. LeCompte, W. L. Millroy and J. Preissle (eds) *The Handbook of Qualitative Research in Education*, pp 447-505, New York, Academic Press

Rooney, E. (1989) *Seductive Reasoning: Pluralism as the Problematic of Contemporary Literary Theory*, Ithaca, NY, Cornell University Press

Smith, D. E. (1987) *The Everyday World as Problematic: A Feminist Sociology,* Boston, Northeastern University Press

Spivak, G. C. (1991) Reflections on Cultural Studies in the Post-colonial Conjuncture: An Interview with the Guest Editor, Cultural Studies: Crossing Boundaries, R. Salper (ed), *Special issue of Critical Studies,* 3(1), pp 63-78

Trinh, T. M-H. (1989) *Woman, Native, Other: Writing Postcoloniality and Feminism,* Bloomington, Indiana University Press

Van Maanen, J. (1988) *Tales of the Field: On Writing Ethnography,* Chicago, University of Chicago Press

5

Feminist Methodology: researching as if gender and social power really mattered

Sharon Grady

Consider: What is your initial response to the word 'feminism'? At IDIERI 2003, members of the Feminist Methodology research station asked all the participants in Jonothan Neelands' drama workshop this question.[1] In a survey we distributed toward the end of our week together, we explicitly asked: 'What does feminism mean to you?' One response, from a young man I'll call Robert, was particularly telling:

> Feminism, at its core, means equal opportunity and ethical treatment for members of both sexes. I essentially agree with feminism, but I sometimes feel intimidated by being researched by feminist researchers. I think my fear is that a random act or decision I make will be seized upon, taken out of context, and used to accuse, try, and convict me as a sexist. The same would be true with any researcher focusing on a single dynamic of a complex event.

There were several subtle and sometimes not so subtle comments and speculations about what our feminist group would produce. For some reason, we made many people very nervous. One Feminist Methodology research station member noted that she was overwhelmed by how we were perceived. 'I have clearly been naive in the past,' she wrote 'I couldn't have believed that a group of women in a group called Feminist Methodology could generate such a reaction.' Where does this nervousness come from? What assumptions were made at IDIERI about what a feminist is and what feminist-inflected research methods might be trying to expose? Weren't we all supposed to be working at 'Destabilising Distinctions and Definitions' as the Institute's focus suggested?

Given such anxiety and resistance, why include a chapter on feminist methodology in a volume such as this? I believe that feminist issues such as gender and access to social power impact on all of us on a daily basis. By extension, our drama work is steeped in it, whether we like it or not. Any drama session can become a text through which we can examine more closely the fictional and real construction of gender and the struggle over social power. But first we have to become more comfortable with the dreaded 'f' word: feminism.

On her website for undergraduate students entitled 'What is Feminism (and why do we have to talk about it so much)?' English professor Mary Klages (1997) posits that the reason for continuing to engage in public conversations about feminism 'has something to do with 'feminism', and even more to do with the history of ideas about gender.' Gender, as most agree, is different from sex. Sex is the biological distinction of being male or female while gender connotes the social distinctions of being masculine or feminine. These distinctions are expressed as a binary (male/female) in which one position (male) is almost always privileged over the other (female). Beyond the obvious social implications, I have argued in the past that this privileging can make a difference in how drama work is conceived, planned, executed, and evaluated (Grady, 2000). But why continue to expend so much time and energy considering gender? Because, as Mary Klages says simply, 'it's there.' And it impacts on every interaction, whether we are conscious of it or not. It's not the only thing that impacts on human interactions, but it is a significant factor and often an invisible or unnoticed one.

Perhaps this discomfort with feminism is less about the notion of gender than, as Klages argues, the fear that any public discussion of gender will necessarily become a discussion about feminism and the potential that we might 'end up saying women are good, men are bad, and it's going to be an excuse to trash men and talk about how white men are horrible oppressors' (1997). This immediately leads us down the slippery slope of politics and the reality of oppression which drama practitioners love to create dramas about but are less comfortable about when it comes to confronting their own actions and practices.

Feminism, like other political movements, seeks to change oppressive structures. It is an oppositional discourse; anytime the *status quo* is challenged, discomfort and resistance ensues. For some, feminism becomes, as American right-wing Christian evangelist Pat Robertson suggests 'a socialist, anti-family, political movement that encourages women to leave their husbands, kill their children, practice witchcraft, destroy capitalism and become lesbians' (Schwartz and Cooper, 1992). Comical as this extreme view may be, there remains a subterranean concern and disquieting fear over what is considered to be a 'feminist agenda' and what changes it might presage for both men and women. Change, whether real or perceived, is scary. And being challenged by ideas that might necessitate changing how we work is alternately seen as truly terrifying or utterly preposterous. 'Will feminism undermine my practice,' you might worry, 'or make me feel that I am inadequate in some way?' 'Look, I'm doing the best I can so give me a break,' you might think. In this light, it's no wonder that the very mention of the word 'feminism' is nothing short of blood-curdling for some.

This chapter seeks to alleviate some of those fears and outline how feminist perspectives on social science research might positively impact on research methods that are applicable to the field of drama/theatre in education. Whilst my own orientation to research is largely informed by a humanities perspective with an emphasis on employing an assortment of critical theories to interpret and analyse how applied drama and theatre 'work' in various contexts, many of us are increasingly placed in situations in which we are asked to justify the 'use value' of our drama-based work by the outcome orientation of the public institutions we are associated with. In the past 25 years, the social sciences have been vigorously challenged by feminist scholars and researchers. Their questions and insights have a great deal to offer us. After establishing a working definition of the difference between feminist methodology and feminist research methods, I examine several core beliefs underpinning a feminist methodology for social science. I then focus on three feminist-nuanced research methods our research station experimented with at IDIERI 2003 and describe how those methods worked together to create larger conversations about the role of gender in small group drama work. Finally, I speculate on how a feminist approach to research methods might be useful for future research.

Feminist methodology

It useful to begin by making a clear distinction between *research methodology*, the theoretical questions that inform our research and how it is done and *research methods*, the actual tools and techniques used to gather evidence, information and data. A feminist research methodology is obviously informed by feminism, which feminist educator and race theorist bell hooks succinctly summarises as 'a movement to end sexism, sexist exploitation, and oppression' (2000, p1). Sociologist Marjorie DeVault argues that a feminist methodology is 'a critique that views the apparatus of knowledge production as one site that has constructed and sustained women's oppression' (1999, p 30). She is clear about the agenda of a feminist methodology in the social sciences:

■ Feminists seek a methodology that will do the work of 'excavation,' shifting the focus of standard practice from men's concerns in order to reveal the locations and perspectives of (all) women

■ Feminists seek a science that minimises harm and control in the research process

■ Feminists seek a methodology that will support research of value to women, leading to social change or action beneficial to women (p 30-31)

This activist agenda is informed by the various articulations of feminism over the years as women have struggled to gain the same rights, power, and opportunities as men. Feminism is often cited as a phenomenon that began with the suffrage movement in the late nineteenth and early twentieth century. This first wave of feminism is marked by the gradual enfranchisement of women in the US and Europe. A second wave can be seen in the late 1960s and early 1970s as consciousness-raising groups drew attention to the importance of women's stories and experience. During this period theories of dominance slowly gave way to theories that included attention to difference and diversity. While some view the present time as the third wave of feminism, because of the increased hybridisation of theory and fragmented understandings of identity, others label this a post-feminist age. For some, this post-feminist era is characterised by the work of popular writers who claim to be feminists yet, as Susan Faludi (1995) points out, spout solidly anti-feminist rhetoric that is clearly supported by conservative backlash interests. For others, such as Frances E. Mascia-Lees and Patricia Sharpe, the term post-feminist indicates the 'context in which the feminism of the 1970s is problematised, splintered, and considered suspect, one in which it is no longer easy, fun, empowering, or even possible, to take a feminist position' (p 3). For them, the post of post-feminism signals the multiplicity of critical concerns feminism has and must take on such areas as post-structuralism, cultural studies, and post-colonialism. In their words: 'feminist ideas are not always depoliticised within post-feminism. They can instead be *differently* politicised' (2000, p 203).

Regardless of how we might name the present articulations of and resistances to feminism, Mary Klages (1997) offers a lengthy but useful set of fundamental feminist attributes:

■ A 'feminist' is someone who is interested in studying and understanding gender as a system of cultural signs or meanings assigned (by various social mechanisms) to sexually-dimorphic bodies, and who sees these cultural signs which constitute gender as having a direct effect on how we live our individual lives and how our social institutions operate

■ Secondly, a 'feminist' is someone who sees the gender systems currently in operation (in our culture and in other cultures) as structured by a basic binary opposition – masculine/feminine – in which one term, masculine, is always privileged over the other term, and that this privileging has had the direct effect of enabling men to occupy positions of social power more often than women. (Note: Not all men are eligible to occupy these positions of power; other binary oppositions are always also at work, such as old/young, or rich/poor, which will mitigate the effect of gender alone; hence a rich old woman might have more forms of social power that a poor young man.) But the basic idea is, if you focus only on the male/female distinction, more men will wield social power (historically and cross-culturally) than women

■ A 'feminist' thinks that points 1 and 2 are wrong and should be changed

Despite the inclusivity implied by Klages' definition, the word feminism continues to conjure a monolithic political or ideological orientation. There are, in fact, multiple articulations of feminism, each with a slightly different agenda. However, whether a feminist is operating from a liberal, radical, materialist, socialist, black, or eco-feminism position the common underpinning is a commitment to redressing sexism. Given the overall agenda of a feminist research methodology, each of these approaches to feminism will yield different research questions and possibly different research methods. Somewhat reassuringly, in her book *Feminist Methods in Social Research*, sociologist Shulamit Reinharz clearly states 'there is no single 'feminist way' to do research' (1992, p 243).

However, many incorrectly assume that a feminist research methodology is primarily associated with qualitative or so-called soft research methods, which are thought to be more closely aligned with a feminist interest in women's experience. Despite, and possibly because of, the troubling gendered assumptions embedded in the hard/soft research binary, methods such as oral history and narrative inquiry seem to naturally associate themselves with a better understanding of the workings of gender through the collection and analysis of stories about women's experience. And, indeed, these methods have yielded valuable feminist research studies. But how can feminists effectively challenge the larger array of research traditions grounded in essentialist or positivist paradigms?

Sociologist Joyce McCarl Nielsen argues that the central assumption behind most research methods, whether qualitative or quantitative in orientation, is a fundamental belief in the *scientific method*, that is a positivist or empirical understanding of how we know what we know (1990, p 1-2). Nielsen notes two main characteristics of this positivist-empirical tradition: rationalism, which is the dominance of pure reason and logic, and empiricism, which is the process of directly observing, recording and monitoring the social and natural world. Researchers are therefore led to believe that the act of doing research is necessarily rational, often impersonal, and largely predictive in scope. Even in the case of qualitative research strategies, attention to triangulation, to a dispassionate interview stance, and a carefully balanced participant/observer mode is suggested. Early feminist challenges to these methodological underpinnings in the social sciences had to do with the inability of feminist researchers, armed with an array of hermeneutic and critical theories, to sustain a dispassionate point of view during interviewing (Oakley, 1981), an acute awareness of the process as well as the statistical 'product' while conducting survey research (Kelly, Regan, and Burton, 1995), and dueling dominant and subversive readings of content analysis (Martin in Reinharz, 1992).[2]

Interestingly, feminist scholars have shown that a sustained belief in positivist-empirical social science research is predominately held by researchers from affluent societies who 'have overwhelming been male, white, able-bodied, heterosexual and 'of a certain maturity'' (Code, 1995, p 15). However, instead of reducing this observation to a simplistic male/female binary, the more interesting question is how have these trends in knowledge production affected what is known and considered knowable? How might a feminist methodology refigure that equation and impact upon our research methods? What happens when we abandon the dispassionate 'view from nowhere', as Code suggests (p 15)?

A close up on three feminist research methods

It isn't just our research questions and the analysis of the data gathered that is influenced by a feminist perspective on research. The method used can also be challenged by paying close attention to the assumptions made about the relationship between the question, the researcher, and the researched in research involving human subjects, how does power circulate and why? The challenges feminist social scientists pose for interview techniques, survey strategies and content analysis have great potential for our research in drama/theatre in education. In each of the following sections, I provide an overview of the method in question, describe how it looks from a feminist social science perspective and pose a few pertinent questions about applications in our own field.

Feminist interviews

Most of us are very familiar with interviewing as a research method. Simply put, the researcher asks questions and gathers answers from people identified as respondents.[3] This transaction might be as brief as five minutes or occur over an extended period of time depending on the research topic. However, interview data is not value free, nor is the process of collecting it. Interviews, as Fontana and Frey (1998) point out, take place 'within the cultural boundaries of a paternalistic social system in which masculine identities are differentiated from female ones' (p 64). Interviewers are generally in a hierarchical relationship with the so-called 'respondent.' To compensate, interviewers have historically been instructed to be even handed but neutral. As Selltiz, Jahoda, Deutsch, and Cook advised in their 1965 volume on *Research Methods in Social Relations*:

> The interviewer's manner should be friendly, courteous, conversational and unbiased. He should be neither too grim nor too effusive; neither too talkative nor too timid. The idea should be to put the respondent at ease so that he will talk freely and fully. (p 576)

While respondents are presumed to be male in this scenario, it is interesting to think about how power impacts on the interview setup if the respondent is female.[4] The possible coerciveness of this dynamic is clearly seen in the structured interview process.

In a structured interview situation, the interviewer asks a number of respondents a series of pre-established questions with a limited set of response categories (Fontana and Frey, 1998, p 52). These interviews often contain a high number of closed questions and are fairly scripted. Because of the imperative to collect the same kinds of data from all respondents, there is very little flexibility. While this mode of interviewing is useful for survey research, respondents might be tempted to provide interviewer-pleasing answers. Given the lack of flexibility in the structured interview process, rewording of questions or adjusting the prescribed mode of address is not possible or advisable. Further, the pre-established question guide often focuses on rational responses and ignores the emotional or contextual dimension of social interactions.

For many feminists using a structured interview format as a research method is complicated. For example, in her important 1981 article 'Interviewing Women: A Contradiction in Terms,' Ann Oakley discusses her interview-based research project on the effects of motherhood on women's lives. For the project she found herself interviewing several pregnant women who had real questions about the process of giving birth. Unwilling to 'play dumb' for purposes of objectivity,

Oakley deviated from her question guide and abandoned her 'cool' stance. Instead, she freely offered answers and unwittingly became friends with her study participants. As a result, she was able to collect remarkably rich interview data. Based on this experience, Oakley encouraged other feminist researchers to give up trying to create the 'illusion' of a clear separation or distance between the researcher and the 'researched'. There can be 'no intimacy without reciprocity', she insists (p 41). Oakley encourages feminist researchers to work at dismantling unequal power dynamics in our research and posits that:

> ... the goal of finding out about people through interviewing is best achieved when the relationship of interviewer and interviewee is non-hierarchical and when the interviewer is prepared to invest his or her own personal identity in the relationship. (1981, p 41)

Oakley suggests that the process of collecting data should be replaced by a process of truly 'interviewing women' in which 'personal involvement is more than dangerous bias-it is the condition under which people come to know each other and to admit others into their lives' (p 58).

The structured interview process certainly highlights questions of power and authority which are key considerations in any feminist-inflected research stance. The issue of the accountability of a researcher to those who have participated in a research project is compelling and not always easy to resolve. As Burt and Code note:

> Feminists are aware that experiences, whether their own or someone else's, rarely speak for themselves; hence they usually require analysis, interpretation. When the inquiry involves speaking for other people or about other people's experiences, there is a tacit consensus among feminists about the responsibility a researcher or writer has to take for the position she occupies and about her accountability to the persons or groups about or for whom she claims to speak. (1995, p 9)

Non-structured interviews can help alleviate some of the problems of the structured interview process. Often designed as an in-depth ethnographic interview experience, the non-structured approach can help a feminist researcher respond to some of the issues Oakley raises. This mode of interviewing thrives on open-ended questions, human-to-human interaction, and a desire to understand rather than to explain. Additionally, Reinharz suggests that semi-structured interviews, in which the researcher 'plans to ask questions about a given topic but allows the data-gathering conversation itself to determine how the information is obtained' (p 281) can help provide greater responsiveness and focus for a feminist inquiry.

What are the implications of Oakley's stance for feminist researchers in our field? While bringing a version of the process-product debate to the realm of research methods has she, as Reinharz (1993) suggests, placed 'excessive demands' on a feminist interviewer? Do you *have* to become friends with your participants? When might such a stance be ill advised? How do the dynamics shift when interviewing small groups of respondents such as students? What happens when a large quantity of data is needed? Can the structured interview process, which has historically been valuable for survey-based research, be rehabilitated?

Feminist survey research

Survey research methods are organised ways to collect data from respondents through questionnaires. The data is then coded and analysed and statistics are derived from the results. From an empirical standpoint, survey research is thought to be a rigorous, scientifically sound method; however, many feminist researchers are ambivalent about the unconditional acceptance of survey research findings and mistrust the prevailing trend for government agencies and funding bodies to rely almost exclusively on survey data. On the other hand, many in our field are now required to provide statistical data about the impact of our work to the various institutional bodies with whom we are affiliated. If we are uneasy with the positivist paradigm that is the bedrock of survey methods, how else might we proceed?

A key component of most survey studies is a questionnaire which is given to a statistically significant number of respondents to gather information. In addition to paper questionnaires, respondents might be surveyed online or through e-mail. Structured face-to-face or telephone interviews, guided by a pre-set series of questions, are often used to gather survey data. Further, secondary data analysis is another useful survey mode in which researchers analyse other people's data such as, government or school statistics. Once gathered, survey data can be coded and analysed in a variety of ways. Large survey projects often benefit from the use of computer software designed specifically to generate questionnaires and to process the data received.

Reinharz (1992) points out that, historically, the use of survey research was connected to the study of social change and social problems. For example, at Hull House, a settlement house for Chicago's poor immigrants established in late 1890s, surveys were key to alleviating social problems or militating for action (p 78). In a present day context, psychologist Toby Jayaratne believes that survey research can help 'counter the pervasive and influential quantitative sexist research which has and continues to be generated in the social sciences' (in Reinharz p 79). She argues that traditional survey procedures can be changed to align with feminist research values and paradigms. For example, as Reinharz suggests, survey research can help describe the breadth and depth of gender-related issues, as well as reveal useful demographic information and reveal links between social institutions and researchers' concerns (p 79-83). In addition, attitudinal surveys can provide information that goes beyond standard behavioural statistics to help understand the perceived meaning of behaviour such as public attitudes about feminism noted earlier.

Feminist researchers Liz Kelly, Linda Regan and Sheila Burton (1995) note that the same charges Oakley levels at the positivist underpinnings of interview research methods such as 'being distanced, objective, keeping to the researcher's agenda, etc. not seeing oneself as a participant in an interaction' can certainly be applied to survey research methods (p 236). 'What makes research feminist is less the method used,' they assert, 'and more how it is used and what it is used for' (p 236). For these researchers, a feminist-inflected approach to their survey-based research project on the prevalence of child sexual abuse allowed them to locate themselves in relation to their research question and their research process.

This British government-funded project relied on young people's willing self-disclosure about sexual victimisation through confidentially administered questionnaires. Although the coding process could have been streamlined if they had chosen to use the format of an American survey on the same subject, the team decided that the responses would have been severely compromised. Instead, they opted for 'open-ended questions where it was inappropriate to offer only predefined options' as a way to provide a context for the respondents' experiences (p 237). Similarly, they decided not to rely solely on the data generated by the surveys but to also keep field notes about each group that responded to the questionnaire, as well as notes about the questions and concerns that arose during their coding process. This mixed approach provided a greater understanding of the complexity of the subject matter and the research process.

However, feminist social scientists are divided on the use value of survey methods. Advocates argue that basing all feminist research efforts on qualitative research will lead to errors. On the other hand, critics of survey research argue that statistical data should be seen as part of patriarchal culture's monolithic reliance on 'hard facts' (Reinharz, 1992, p 87). A key concern that frequently emerges is that survey research cannot adequately take into account context and diversity. Further, survey studies are seen to be dependent on definitive responses to biased questions. What results, Betty Gray argues, is a 'statistical-industrial complex' that colludes to disguise problems and issues which reinforces sexism via statistics (in Reinharz p 87). Some even argue that gathering data in this way can be a convenient way to avoid taking action. These concerns have led some feminist researchers to strongly advocate combining survey methods with other approaches.

As a researcher who has often used informal surveys as a way to gather preliminary information prior to an extended interview, several questions about feminist survey methods remain. How can we best use survey methods for feminist purposes in our field? How can a researcher avoid reproducing sexist or reductive survey questions or results? What other methods might be used in tandem with survey studies to address the complexity of our research questions? How can we read the results of our survey data through a feminist lens?

Feminist content analysis

Broadly, content analysis is the study of things 'using the discourse of person as commentary upon them' (Martineau in Reinharz, 1992, p 145). In its most formal incarnation, content analysis has become known as a research method used to determine the presence or frequency of particular words or concepts within a single text or group of texts. Typically, content analysis researchers count and then analyse these words and concepts. Finally, they make inferences about the 'messages' or meanings available within and between the texts, the writers, the audience, and even the culture and time to which the objects in question belong. Following a post-structural understanding of what constitutes a text, the objects for investigation are endless, from anything containing a written word to any spoken utterance to any single image or collection of signs. To conduct a content analysis, the researcher dismantles the text and divides it into smaller component parts, specific words, themes, gestures, etc., and then examines the pieces more closely using either a conceptual form of analysis or a relational one. A conceptual analysis helps establish the existence and frequency of concepts, most often represented by words or phrases, in a text. In contrast, a relational analysis goes one step further by examining the relationships among or between concepts in a text.

From a feminist perspective, Reinharz contends that 'people who do content analyses study a set of objects (i.e., cultural artifacts) or events systematically by counting them or interpreting the themes contained in them' (1992, p 146). Whilst once again a positivist proposition, content analysis can be highly useful for feminist research. As Reinharz says:

> Typically, studying cultural products through the lens of feminist theory exposes a pervasive patriarchal and even misogynist culture. Sometimes these cultural themes are found even when feminist literature is the object... On the other hand, some cultural artifacts oppose the dominant culture. (1992, p 147)

Reinharz posits two characteristics of cultural artifacts:

1. they possess a naturalistic, 'found' quality because they are not created for the purpose of study (i.e. written records, journals, etc)

2. they are noninteractive, i.e., they do not require asking questions of respondents or observing live behaviour (i.e. interview transcripts, videos, etc.)

From a feminist perspective, content analysis is largely a deconstructive exercise. The researcher is looking closely at what is present as well as analysing what is missing which Reinharz calls 'the sociology of the lack of knowledge' (1992, p163). Not surprisingly, both quantitative and qualitative methods can be utilised in this endeavour. The most used quantitative methods having to do with accounting and include word and/or phrase counts to determine frequency which can help identify patterns of authorship, subject matter, methods, and interpretation. These findings are then used to generate or test hypotheses relevant to feminist theory and concerns, or to press for social change (Reinharz, 1992, p 155).

Qualitative methods often include the use of an inductive or interpretive framework through which to analyse a cultural milieu. We can, for example, analyse texts for preferred or dominant readings and then reread them in 'subversive ways'. Organisational scientist Joanne Martin provides an intriguing example of this process. In her 1990 article, 'Deconstructing Organisational Taboos: The Suppression of Gender Conflict in Organisations,' Martin relates a story told by a corporate executive in a conference setting about a female employee 'who is extraordinarily important' to the launch of a new product, who 'has arranged to have her Caesarean yesterday in order to be prepared for this event' but whom they have insisted should be 'staying home three months' and for whom they 'are finding ways of filling in to create this void for us because we think it's an important thing for her to do'. This small excerpt of corporate 'double-speak' readily lends itself to multiple readings, as Martin explains:

> I deconstruct and reconstruct this story from a feminist viewpoint, examining what it says, what it does not say, and what it might have said. This analysis highlights suppressed gender conflicts implicit in this story and shows how apparently well-intentioned organizational practices can reify, rather than alleviate, gender inequalities. (In Reinharz, 1992, p 149)

This framework can be used to review everything from public historical documents and personal papers to contemporary cultural artifacts. I believe drama work represents a kind of cultural artifact that can be submitted to similar scrutiny by feminist researchers. We can, for example, critically assess a transcript of a drama session, a video tape of a dramatic episode, a lesson plan, or even the pre-text from which a drama is initiated. This deep analysis of content can make visible gender-related issues that may be overlooked in the throes of doing drama work and can aid practitioners in their attempts at creating more equitable environments in which drama work can happen.

But how do we best organise the accounting aspect associated with articulations of this method? What frameworks or rubrics might help in understanding or analysing what we see? Can counting alone provide satisfying data? How does the 'sociology of lack' operate in our field? How might we most productively frame and deconstruct a moment of drama-based work as a cultural artifact?

How did feminist research methods work at IDIERI 2003?

To grapple with some of the challenges posed by feminist interview, survey, and content analysis methods, members of the Feminist Methodology research station immediately set about the task of creating a suitable research question that would help us focus our experiments. After viewing Neelands's initial workshop session based on Antigone, we discussed what struck us about the work and the ways in which the Institute framed these demonstration sessions. From our impressions, we brainstormed research topics that might be interesting to pursue from a feminist perspective. Initial ideas included body language, group talk, the relationship between process and outcome, types of contracts and drama strategies that empower or disempower participants, the degree to which the participants are conscious of our feminist perspective, the power/authority of the leader, and the relationship between gender dynamics and group work. We concluded that these topics generally fell into three large categories: group dynamics, leadership issues and content. We then drafted a research question we felt we could handle given our short time together: 'What are the ways in which decisions are made individually and in small groups? What does gender have to do with it?' As we began our work, this two-part question was further refined: 'How might gender impact the ways in which decisions are made individually and in small groups?'

Experimenting with feminist interviews

We began exploring our research question through feminist semi-structured interviews. Despite the rapid-fire pace of the Institute, at our second meeting we managed to take a few minutes to identify some relevant areas of interest we wanted to discuss and craft a few interview questions before we were given access to some of the drama participants. We quickly divided into three working groups and were able to interview a total of ten participants. Each group of researchers quickly adjusted to the spontaneous interview format.

One team, for example, sat in a circle and interspersed a small group of respondents amongst them. Another group sat in a circle and interviewed their respondents one at a time.

However, three incidents revealed some key issues that need to be taken into account when conducting feminist interviews. First, our zeal for the task at hand led to an alarming incident with a young male respondent who seemed uncomfortable as he walked in for his solo interview with a group of four female researchers. He immediately turned his chair around and sat splayed with his arms planted firmly on the top of the back of the chair for the duration of the interview. At one point he stopped the interview and asked if he could ask a question: 'Why are you doing that with your hair? Are you being a girlie or something?' This was directed at one of our researchers who wore a low-cut pink dress and pink flowery sandals that day. After an awkward exchange, the moment turned out to be an interesting comment on how gender is performed, both his and ours, how gender is read, and what gender expectations have to do with social interactions such as an interview situation.

The researcher later reflected on the incident:

> I thought it was hugely funny when someone said that he obviously thought I'd got my clothes and shoes out of the props cupboard and was there as a plant! It was an eye opener to others' perceptions of feminism, the suspicion, the threat felt by this particular young man. Also I was made very aware of the role of the interviewer. I hadn't before considered the messages conveyed by the questioner. How do we come across, Investigator? Interrogator? Facilitator for a bigger question unknown and undivulged? I did leave that session quite disturbed. I felt very exposed in pink – and paranoid about my habit of touching my hair ...

The second incident arose the following day as we shared stories about how each of the interview groups functioned and pondered our results. A Korean researcher in our research station confessed that she felt utterly silenced during the interview process because of her struggles with English – and this upset her. We spent a good deal of time grappling with how, for all our sensitivity to our respondents' experience of the interview process, we forgot to look more carefully at our own group dynamics and issues of equity.

Reflecting on this, another research station member commented in her journal:

> I had felt excited and enthused from the interviewing and was brought back down to earth by her comments. I had sensed her quiet during and after the interviews and we had conversed after the interviews about our potential impact on [the respondent's] behaviour, etc. but I hadn't taken her sense of the experience on board. Instead, I was swept along with my, and others, excitement at common questions and perceptions...a valuable learning experience in essentialism? She had not felt that the questions we asked were common. We had not fully negotiated. She was positioned as observer without consent.

Finally, as part of the interviewing component of our research work, we were able to send one representative to interview Neelands for five minutes. In this interview, Neelands revealed that he decided not to make small group dynamics a central focus of his teaching at the Institute, which caused our group to debate the relative value of continuing with our inquiry. There was particular concern over a question we were developing for our questionnaire about the leader's role in creating productive and equitable group dynamics. After much debate, we were mostly in agreement that regardless of Neelands' comments our inquiry was valid. This conversation pointed to the tempting research pitfall of locating a definitive understanding of the truth of a group experience, such as drama work, in the comments of only one respondent, even if that respondent is the drama leader.

Experimenting with feminist survey research

Our research station embarked on two types of feminist survey approaches:

- a written questionnaire that featured a variety of question types (see Appendix A)

- a visual survey that featured line drawings the respondents could circle as attitudinal indicators of their drama experience at IDIERI (see Appendix B).

In my previous survey experiments I had tabulated the results by hand. For the Institute, however, I was curious how Mac-friendly survey software might aid in both the creation and tabulation of survey results. While there are many programmes available for PC users, in the summer of 2003 I found only two available user-friendly Mac products. I decided to try Power Knowledge's PowerTab product which is aimed at non-survey specialists like those of us in the Feminist Methodology research station. The software is designed to enable users with little or no statistical experience to create and interpret surveys with relative ease.[5]

Working with PowerTab helped us expand our understandings of common survey question types. These included:

■ Single response (respondents choose yes/no or other fixed choice)

■ Multi response (respondents select all that apply)

■ Numeric open-end response (respondents enter/tell you a number)

■ Text open-end response (respondents enter/tell textual information as an open response)

■ Group-rating scale (respondents rate various aspects of an item on a six point scale, best to no opinion; strongly agree to strongly disagree, etc.)

We were able to incorporate all of these question types into the written survey. However, as Kelly, Regan and Burton (1995) noted, ease of coding was sacrificed to the need to offer two open-ended textual responses in order to more fully address our research question and our concerns about process. Further, the conditions under which these surveys were created, framed, and administered proved to be quite stressful for the researchers and respondents. But although the artificial nature of conducting research at the Institute compromised the quality of the research experience for both groups, the written questionnaire netted fascinating results.

The first eight questions had to do with basic drama and demographic concerns, such as prior experience with drama and/or Neelands, age, country of residence, languages spoken, economic circumstances, gender, and education. We then asked the respondents to consider if they self-identified more as an extrovert or an introvert, the degree to which the fishbowl effect of the Institute affected them, and how easy or difficult it was for them to share their opinions during the large group and small group work. Respondents were also asked to rate their level of participation, ability to collaborate, sensitivity to other group members, as well as their ability to build on others' ideas, provide leadership, and be a follower. The final section dealt most specifically with gender issues and group dynamics and asked the respondents if they had a gender preference for co-workers in small group work, if gender played a role in their group work at IDIERI, and what the role of a drama leader was in creating equitable group dynamics. The final question asked about their response to the word 'feminism' and what it means to them.

There were seven men and five women respondents to our written survey. In terms of self-concept, all the women reported that, depending on context, they could be either an extrovert or an introvert, whereas only four of the men did. Of the others, one self-identified as an extrovert, one as an introvert, and one chose not to answer the question. Offering opinions in the large group setting was 'fairly easy' for four of the women and 'very easy' for one. For the men, three found it 'very easy' while two found it 'fairly easy' to share their opinions in the large group. Equally, two of the men found it 'sometimes hard to share' opinions in the large group setting. However, in the small group work, five of the men found it 'very easy' to share their opinions, against only two of the women. Instead, three of the women found it 'fairly easy' to share opinions in the small group. Both men and women rated their levels of participation and ability to collaborate fairly high. Interestingly, all the women rated their sensitivity to other group members' needs as 'very good' whereas only two of the men did so. In fact, three of the men thought they were 'outstandingly' sensitive while two felt they were 'average'. Both genders felt they built on others' ideas very well. However, two of the women felt they were 'very good' at providing leadership, two of them felt they were only fair, with one rating herself average. By contrast, four of the men felt they were 'very good' at providing leadership with only one rating himself as only fair.

Although the small group gender balance question was worded in a way that didn't net useful results, in response to the question: 'Do you find it easier to work with a small group made up mostly of people of your sex?' one young man indicated that 'it doesn't matter to me' but added in the margin: 'With the feminist group looking on, I was always self conscious about being perceived as adopting a traditional paternalistic male role.' In the specific case of the small group work at IDIERI, three of the women felt everyone contributed equally while three of the men did. One woman felt that men tended to answer more often than women and three of the men agreed with one commenting that men tended to take more leadership than women. Interestingly, one man wrote in the margin: 'Overall, I think it was even. But I fear the feminist group was ready to pounce on any moment in which a male lead out and may have missed moments where a female lead out.'

Experimenting with feminist content analysis

Our feminist content analysis work gave us some interesting ways to look at how each of the actual drama sessions might be read as a text. Some of our researchers read a particular session as if it was a script and carefully analysed the leader's content and structural choices. One recorded:

> Observation informs the teacher's awareness of the group and scrutinising JN's sessions with a feminist methodological per-spective had this same effect for me in terms of potentially in-forming my own practice. At one point in his 2nd session, three characters had become the focus: Pedro, a teacher and a visitor to the school. In this instance, all three characters were male and the narrative had taken a specific turn the group had identified the values of the society in the drama as athleticism, competition and made multiple references to football. I was contemplating the extent to which teachers', gendered?, choice of material im-pacts upon participants.

Another group of feminist researchers chose to conduct content analysis research on specific moment in one of the sessions in which Neelands asked for the participants to demonstrate the qualities of a superhero with a gesture. The researchers reviewed the video of that moment and created a rubric through which to analyse each parti-cipant's movement, including the size of gesture, space needed, levels used, facial expression, speed, and strength of the gesture. Their use of voice was also analysed, including volume, tone, and speed as well as use of language, including the quality of sound, harsh/soft, and content, internal/external, intellectual, verbal, physical, emotional.

Still another of our feminist researchers chose to collect statistical evidence about who took ownership of the pen when drama participants were asked to write down ideas in small groups. The evidence seemed to support the subjective observations made by other feminist observers with regard to apparent male dominance. She writes:

> The students were asked to form four groups and were given a large piece of paper and one pen. They were all read an essay, which had apparently been written by a child and entered for an essay writing competition by his school. The students were asked to write on the paper what could be decoded about the child, the teacher, the school and the society as depicted in the essay. I noted the gender of the person who picked up the pen in each group, thereby giving themselves potential control over exactly what was to be written on the paper, a dominant role in the group.

Group no.	No. males	No. females	Who 'owned' the pen
1	2	2	male
2	2	2	male
3	1	3	female
4	3	1	male

The only group where a female picked up the pen was in Group 3 which had more females in it than males. In all the other groups, males chose the pen, and the position it gave them.

That a feminist methodology research station was busily engaged in conducting research experiments at IDIERI profoundly affected perceptions about feminism and put everyone on high alert regarding gender dynamics and access to social power. If feminism is about paying attention to gender relations, was this heightened state of alert and its accompanying discomfort necessarily a bad thing? I don't think so. Perhaps for the first time, gender became a live issue for many of the Institute's participants. In all, I feel our small efforts to enact several different feminist research methods at IDIERI proved quite successful. Whether counting frequency, or analysing a video tape of a particular moment for body and vocal comfort, deconstructing a transcript of a drama-based lesson, or interviewing an individual or a group of drama participants, or surveying verbally and visually, a feminist approach to research has much to offer the field.

Implications for future research

On our last day together at IDIERI, one researcher had a breakthrough moment during a discussion about destabilising the notions of validity and triangulation. I mentioned that the cautions and concerns over skewing the data if member checking wasn't rigorously pursued was based in a positivist understanding of truth being locatable as long as it wasn't contaminated. However, it can be much more interesting if triangulation and member checking yields a plethora of opinion. Personally, I'm more interested in why people see things in such different ways rather than whether they all agree. This flies in the face of conventional positivist wisdom and the researcher announced that her head was ready to explode. Her head is, thankfully, still intact, but this interaction points to a productive path for reconfiguring our future research agendas and designs.

Besides our collective excitement about the potential feminist-inflected research holds for future collaborative investigations, several of our researchers shared thoughts about how the work might influence their future work. For example, a researcher believes that a feminist approach to research is not merely another tool to be co-opted and used:

> For me, feminist literary theory, feminist theory and theatre, feminist research methodologies in connection with education are a *part* of the field, not just useful to the field. For others, a feminist perspective was not one they had considered in the way that I had. This, in itself, was an interesting start point.

Another researcher believes a feminist lens aids in foregrounding gender issues and recognition of inequities. She is passionate about the ways in which feminist research methods can enrich the field as well as advocate for social action:

> I feel that this sort of research is especially useful for teacher research that engages both teacher/director/leader and students/actors/participants in recognising unexamined assumptions and perpetuation of stereotypes in the work they do together, again for the ultimate enlightenment and positioning of

all as better able to recognise what's needed and to work toward a more just society.

Similarly, yet another researcher believes that feminist-influenced research can provide a clear counter distinction to government lists and tick boxes:

> In Feminist methodology we are wondering what takes place beneath the surface. There are no such lists of what we should expect to find – what a child should have achieved. We are not concerned with tests that apparently measure and tell. So the mode is working against a familiar mode of looking into the educational context, and this makes it useful as a method of research for the field. It counters the contemporary obsession with measuring.

A feminist perspective on research methods has the potential to challenge received understandings of what constitutes research and how it is pursued. It encourages us to embrace research strategies that are less concerned with the orderliness of a positivist paradigm and instead pay closer attention to ruptures and disjunctures. It encourages us to strive to rehabilitate useful positivist methods such as survey research, and embrace the collaborative and interactive potential of a feminist methodology in our field. Of course, researchers who choose to take up this oppositional challenge may encounter resistance. However, the need to continue destabilising definitions and distinctions is vital. Perhaps a renewed feminist commitment to researching as if gender relations and access to social power really mattered will help in those efforts.

Notes

1 Names of respondents have been changed to maintain anonymity.

2 While it could be argued that this simple characterisation of a positivist research mode sets up yet another binary and that available research paradigms are multiple and various, as I have argued elsewhere (Grady, 1996), understanding how qualitative and quantitative approaches can be considered part and parcel of the same paradigmatic package is useful – especially given that the end goal of most social science research is to control and predict behaviour. How often are we put in the position of being accountable for similar outcomes when evaluating our work in the elementary and secondary sectors?

3 Because of the implied power dynamics between the researcher and the 're-searched', the term 'respondent' is a problematic one for feminist researchers. But, as Reinharz wonders:

Is the interviewee a participant? A subject? An informant? This variety reflects the fact that feminist research methods are both rooted in the mainstream disciplines and represent a protest against them. Using unconventional terms such as 'participant' instead of 'subject' is a signal that the researcher is operating in a feminist framework that includes the power to name or rename. (1992, p 22)

4   Certainly another version of this problem continues to be considered in educational research when adults interview young people.

5   PowerTab supports paper and web questionnaires and can tabulate from Filemaker Pro databases if desired. Although it features an 'Expert Helper' designed more for American small business concerns than feminist researchers, a user can easily design original surveys from a fairly simple editor window. The software allows for multiple response data and will produce data results in a tidy table format. In addition, it will allow you to cross-reference your data and chart it (i.e. data from two question categories – such as age and gender, or gender and self-concept, etc.). As a novice at developing more complex surveys to gather relatively sophisticated data, I was very pleased. (For more information, visit www.powerknowledge.com)

Recommended Readings and Resources

Introductory Readings

DeVault, Marjorie (1999) What is feminist methodology?/Talking Back to Sociology: Distinctive Contributions of Feminist Methodology. In *Liberating Method: Feminism and Social Research*, Philadelphia, Temple University Press, p 21-45

DeVault, Marjorie (1999) Craft Knowledge of Feminist Research/From the Seminar Room: Practical Advice for Researchers. In *Liberating Method: Feminism and Social Research*, Philadelphia, Temple University Press, p 193-231

The Feminist Interview

Reinharz, Shulamit (1992) Feminist Interview Research. In *Feminist Methods in Social Research, Oxford*, Oxford University Press, p 18-45

Feminist Survey Research

Kelly, Liz, Regan, L. and Burton, S. (1995) 'Defending the Indefensible? Quantitative Methods and Feminist Research'. Holland, J., Blair, M. w/ Sheldon S. (eds.) *Debates and Issues in Feminist Research and Pedagogy*, Clevedon, UK, Multilingual Matters LTD, p235-247

Feminist Content Analysis

Reinharz, Shulamit (1992) Feminist Content Analysis. In *Feminist Methods in Social Research*, Oxford, Oxford University Press, p 145-163

Web Resources for Feminist Theory and Research

Feminist Theory Website, http://www.cddc.vt.edu/feminism/

Feminist and Women's Journals, http://www.feminist.org/research/pubjourn.html

Stanford Encyclopedia of Philosophy: Introduction to Feminism: http://www.mit.edu/~shaslang/papers/femintro.html

References

An Introduction to Content Analysis. [online]. Available from: http://writing.colostate.edu/references/research/content/pop2a.cfm [Accessed on 09/06/03]

Brayton, Jennifer (1997) What makes Feminist Research Feminist? The Structure of Feminist Research with the Social Sciences [online]. Available at: http://www.unb.ca/web/PAR-L/win/feminmethod.htm [Accessed on: 25/05/03]

Burt, Sandra and Code, Lorraine (eds.) (1995) *Changing Methods: Feminists Transforming Practice*, Toronto, Broadview Press

Code, Lorraine (1995) How Do We Know? Questions of Method in Feminist Practice. In Burt, S. and Code L. (eds.), *Changing Methods: Feminists Transforming Practice*, Toronto, Broadview Press, p 13-43

DeVault, Marjorie (1999) *Liberating Method: Feminism and Social Research*, Philadelphia, Temple University Press

Faludi, Susan (1995) I'm not a Feminist, But I play one on TV. *Ms. Magazine* (March/April), p 30-39

Fletcher, Helen (1995) Retrieving the Mother/Other from the Myths and Margins of O'Neill's 'Seal Wife' Drama. *NADIE Journal*, 19 (2), p 25-38

Fontana, Andrea and Frey, James H. (1998) Interviewing: The Art of Science. In Denzin, Norman and Lincoln, Yvonne (eds.), *Collecting and Interpreting Qualitative Materials,* Thousand Oaks, CA, SAGE Publications, p 47-78

Grady, Sharon (2000) *Drama and Diversity: A Pluralistic Perspective for Educational Drama*, Portsmouth, NH, Heinemann

Grady, Sharon (1996) Toward the Practice of Theory in Practice. In Taylor, P. (ed.), *Researching Drama and Arts Education: Paradigms and Possibilities*, London, Falmer

hooks, bell (2000) *Feminism is for Everybody: Passionate Politics*, Cambridge, MA, South End Press

Kelly, Liz, Regan, L. and Burton, S. (1995) Defending the Indefensible? Quantitative Methods and Feminist Research. In Holland, J., Blair, M. w/ Sheldon S. (eds.) *Debates and Issues in Feminist Research and Pedagogy*, Clevedon, UK, Multilingual Matters LTD, p 235-247

Klages, Mary (1997) What is Feminism (and why do we have to talk about it so much)? [online]. Available from: www.colorado.edu/English/ENGL2012Klages/1feminism.html [Accessed 06/06/03]

Mascia-Lees, Frances and Sharpe, Patricia (2000) *Taking a Stand in a Post-feminist World: Toward an Engaged Cultural Criticism*, Albany, NY, State University of New York Press

Nielsen, Joyce McCarl (ed.) (1990) *Feminist Research Methods: Exemplary Readings in the Social Sciences*, Boulder, CO, Westview Press

Oakley, A. (1981). Interviewing women: A contradiction in terms. In Roberts, H. (ed.), *Doing Feminist Research*, London, Routledge and Kegan Paul, p 30-61

Reinharz, Shulamit (1992) *Feminist Methods in Social Research*, Oxford, Oxford University Press

Reinharz, Shulamit (1993) Neglected Voices and Excessive Demands in Feminist Research, *Qualitative Sociology* 16(1), p 69-75

Schwartz, Maralee and Cooper, Kenneth (1992) 'Equal Rights Initiative in Iowa Attacked' [FINAL Edition] *The Washington Post*, Washington, D.C., Aug 23, pa.15

Selltiz, C. Jahoda, M., Deutsch, M., and Cook, S. W. (1965) *Research Methods in Social Relations*, London, Methuen

APPENDIX A
IDIERI 2003 — ASKING THE PARTICIPANTS!
THANK YOU ALL SO MUCH FOR AGREEING TO COMPLETE THIS
QUESTIONNAIRE FOR THE FEMINIST METHODOLOGIES RESEARCH STATION.
WE HAVE BEEN ATTEMPTING TO CONSIDER THE NATURE OF GROUP
DYNAMICS IN DRAMA WORK AND YOUR OPINIONS ARE VERY IMPORTANT TO
US.
THE FIRST PART OF THE QUESTIONNAIRE ASKS YOU A BIT MORE ABOUT
YOURSELF. THE SECOND PART DELVES INTO ISSUES RELATED TO
GROUP DYNAMICS.
THANKS!

1.   HAVE YOU EVER PARTICIPATED IN A DRAMA WORKSHOP QUITE LIKE
     THIS BEFORE?
     YES. 1   NO. 2

2.   HAVE YOU EVER WORKED WITH JONOTHAN NEELAND'S BEFORE?
     YES. 1   NO. 2

3.   WHICH OF THE FOLLOWING CATEGORIES CONTAINS YOUR AGE?
     18 or Younger. 1   36-40. 6
     19-21. 2   41-45. 7
     22-25. 3   46-50. 8
     26-30. 4   51-60. 9
     31-35. 5   60 or More. 10

4.   WHICH OF THE FOLLOWING BEST DESCRIBES YOUR COUNTRY OR
     PLACE OF RESIDENCE?
     AUSTRALIA. 1   SCOTLAND. 5
     CANADA. 2   SINGAPORE. 6
     ENGLAND. 3   WALES. 7
     IRELAND. 4   UNITED STATES OF AMERICA. 8

5.   WHICH OF THE FOLLOWING LANGUAGES DO YOU FEEL CONFIDENT
     SPEAKING?
     (Check all that apply.)
     ENGLISH. 1   CHINESE. 7
     FRENCH. 2   MANDARIN. 8
     SPANISH. 3   JAPANESE. 9
     GERMAN 4   SWEDISH. 10
     HINDI. 5   DUTCH. 11
     URDU. 6   OTHER (Please List):. 12

6.   WHICH CATEGORY BEST DESCRIBES THE ECONOMIC
     CIRCUMSTANCES IN WHICH YOU GREW UP?
     POOR. 1   UPPER MIDDLE CLASS. 4
     WORKING CLASS. 2   UPPER CLASS. 5
     MIDDLE CLASS. 3   WEALTHY. 6

7.   ARE YOU...
      FEMALE?. 1   MALE? 2

8.   PLEASE INDICATE WHICH CATEGORY BEST DESCRIBES YOUR
      EDUCATIONAL SITUATION:
      SOME COLLEGE COURSES AT THE UNDERGRADUATE LEVEL, NO
      DEGREE YET. 1
      HAVE UNDERGRAD DEGREE, NOT PURSUING GRAD OR POST-GRAD
      WORK 2
      PURSUING A POST GRADUATE DEGREE IN DRAMA (MA, MFA, PGCE,
      ETC.). 3
      PURSUING A DOCTORAL DEGREE (PHD). 4
      OTHER (Please Explain) 5

9.   WHICH OF THE FOLLOWING STATEMENTS BEST DESCRIBES YOU:
      I AM AN EXTREME EXTROVERT. . . 1   I AM AN INTROVERT 4
      I AM AN EXTROVERT. 2   I AM AN EXTREME INTROVERT. 5
      DEPENDING ON THE CONTEXT, I CAN BE EITHER AN EXTROVERT OR
      AN INTROVERT 3

10.   TO WHAT DEGREE DID HAVING THE 'AUDIENCE' OBSERVING YOUR
      WORKSHOPS CONTRIBUTE TO HOW YOU CHOSE TO PARTICIPATE IN
      THE DRAMA?
      DIDN'T BOTHER ME AT ALL!—I DIDN'T NOTICE YOU!. 1
      BOTHERED ME A BIT—BUT I TRIED TO FORGET YOU WERE THERE. . 2
      BOTHERED ME—I FELT LIKE I WAS UNDER A MICROSCOPE.. 3
      REALLY BOTHERED ME—MADE IT HARD TO CONCENTRATE. 4
      BOTHERED ME A LOT!—I FELT I WAS PERFORMING FOR YOU.. 5
      OTHER RESPONSES:. 6

11.   WHICH OF THE FOLLOWING STATEMENTS BEST DESCRIBES HOW
      EASY OR DIFFICULT IT WAS TO OFFER YOUR OPINIONS IN THE LARGE
      GROUP DRAMA WORK:
          IT WAS VERY EASY TO SHARE MY OPINIONS 1
          IT WAS FAIRLY EASY TO SHARE MY OPINIONS. 2
          IT WAS SOMETIMES HARD TO SHARE MY OPINIONS. 3
          IT WAS FAIRLY DIFFICULT FOR ME TO SHARE MY OPINIONS. 4
          IT WAS VERY DIFFICULT FOR ME TO SHARE MY OPINIONS. 5

12. WHICH OF THE FOLLOWING STATEMENTS BEST DESCRIBES HOW EASY OR
DIFFICULT IT WAS TO OFFER YOUR OPINIONS IN THE SMALL GROUP DRAMA
WORK:
          IT WAS VERY EASY TO SHARE MY OPINIONS 1
          IT WAS FAIRLY EASY TO SHARE MY OPINIONS. 2
          IT WAS SOMETIMES HARD TO SHARE MY OPINIONS. 3
          IT WAS FAIRLY DIFFICULT FOR ME TO SHARE MY OPINIONS. 4
          IT WAS VERY DIFFICULT FOR ME TO SHARE MY OPINIONS. 5

13.   CONSIDERING THE VARIOUS DRAMA SESSIONS, HOW WOULD RATE
        YOURSELF ON THE FOLLOWING:
        OUTSTANDING VERY GOOD AVERAGE FAIR POOR
        1 2 3 4 5
        1. LEVEL OF PARTICIPATION. . . . .
        2. ABILITY TO COLLABORATE. . . . .
        3. SENSITIVITY TO OTHER GROUP MEMBERS' NEEDS. . . . .
        4. BUILDING ON OTHERS' IDEAS. . . . .
        5. ABILITY TO PROVIDE LEADERSHIP. . . . .
        6. ABILITY TO BE A FOLLOWER. . . . .

14.   DO YOU FIND IT EASIER TO WORK WITH A SMALL GROUP MADE UP
        OF MORE PEOPLE OF YOUR SAME SEX RATHER THAN LESS?
        YES!. 1   IT'S NEVER OCCURRED TO ME. 4
        NO. 2   WHY? (Please Comment). 5
        IT DOESN'T MATTER TO ME. 3

15.   WE ARE INTERESTED IN WHETHER OR NOT GENDER PLAYED A ROLE
        IN HOW GROUP WORK UNFOLDED. HOW WOULD YOU
        CHARACTERISE THE PREDOMINANT GENDER DYNAMIC IN YOUR
        GROUP WORK?
        WOMEN TENDED TO COMMENT MORE OFTEN THAN MEN.. 1
        WOMEN TENDED TO TAKE MORE LEADERSHIP ROLES THAN MEN.. .2
        EVERYONE CONTRIBUTED EQUALLY.. 3
        MEN TENDED TO ANSWER MORE OFTEN THAN WOMEN.. 4
        MEN TENDED TO TAKE MORE LEADERSHIP ROLES THAN WOMEN.. .5
        COMMENTS?. 6

16.   WHAT IS THE ROLE OF THE DRAMA LEADER IN CREATING
        EQUITABLE GROUP DYNAMICS?

17.   WHAT IS YOUR INITIAL RESPONSE TO THE WORD 'FEMINISM'? WHAT
        DOES IT MEAN TO YOU?

18.   WE WOULD LOVE TO TALK OR CORRESPOND MORE ABOUT YOUR
        EXPERIENCES IN THIS WORKSHOP. IF YOU WOULD BE INTERESTED,
        PLEASE WRITE YOUR NAME AND EMAIL INFORMATION BELOW.
        THANKS!

Appendix B.

6

Narrative Inquiry: Postcards from Northampton

Belarie Zatzman

What is narrative inquiry?

I begin with questions. Beware – I end with questions too. I have been collecting questions about narrative inquiry, in response to my encounter with narrative research adopted in a range of forms across disciplinary boundaries. Even within a single discipline, narrative might be employed differently, so definitions are difficult from the outset. Fundamentally however, narrative inquiry suggests that we all live storied lives. In excavating narrative inquiry as a research methodology, we can begin to discover the ways in which narrative provides a means of making sense of one's own experiences, particularly as the narrator/ performer unpacks a story that is located within her or his culture, language, gender, and history.

Narrative inquiry asks us to retell our stories as research and to examine those stories critically. If we understand that we participate in the construction of our own narrative(s), this research methodology can affect how we view education, our conception of the role of the teacher, and how we create drama and theatre within and beyond our classroom walls. In both drama education and narrative inquiry, we understand that identity is situational and narratives of the self are embodied. Narrative research has a propensity to place the autobiographical at the centre of its investigation. Narrative inquiry can provide a process for constructing and rehearsing our own identities, situating them amongst the narratives of others present and past.

In lieu of a definition for narrative as a research methodology, Clandinin and Connelly (2000) take up the challenge of articulating what 'narrative inquirers do'. Central to their examination is their conception of a metaphoric, three-dimensional narrative inquiry space. Within this space, researchers can begin to both assemble and question the boundaries of their inquiry (pp 49-51). It is a narrative framework which asks researchers to contemplate three essential elements of their inquiry landscape: a) personal/ social issues; b) temporal issues; c) issues of location. The intersection and complexity of this triad is made manifest in this reflection:

> Throughout her narrative inquiry, she remains in her Canadian place while traveling back in time and place, in memory, to a China that no longer exists. The three-dimensional space in which her research is situated creates an ongoing sense of dislocation as she moves from a remembered past in one place to a present moment in another, all the while imaginatively constructing an identity for the future. (Clandinin and Connelly, 2000, p 55)

Conle's (2003) contribution to the discussion of narrative inquiry as a research methodology is useful in its account of an 'anatomy of narrative curricula'. She describes 'practices that view narrative research activities as curricular activities' (p 3), including narrative curricula that give rise to explicit, tacit and/ or practical learning. From narrative inquiry as curricular experience (e.g., in graduate courses/thesis work), to narrative inquiry as performative/ performance (e.g., the representation of data in art forms), to narratively oriented teacher education (e.g., stories as case study), Conle outlines the range, significance and application of narrative methodologies. She asserts that because narrative is 'pervasive in everyday life, it can create the bridges between the everyday and the academic world that, for example, John Dewey (1938) had in mind' (p 13). Conle suggests:

> When inquiry touches issues intimately connected to one's life, learning becomes all-important, as important as practicing their art is to committed musicians, painters, or poets. Like these endeavors,

> narrative curricula highlight the importance of the moment-the ex-
> perience of the moment and what happens in encounters with
> people and things, moment by moment. (p 13)

In structuring narrative inquiry, one might also recall Britzman's caution that rather than representing our real selves in contemporary research methodologies, we create 'textualised identities' (2003, p 244). It behoves us to acknowledge and question the sometimes contradictory interpretations of our narratives, the forms of representation, and our practices of reflexivity in inquiry. Just as post-structuralists read the absent against the present (p 245), so narrative inquiry asks us to read our narratives as layers of time and place, in which 'every telling is constrained, partial, and determined by the discourses and histories that prefigure, even as they might promise, representation' (p 247). Thus, over time our narrative statements, and the forms that acts of narrating take, may change 'the story of the narrator during the telling of the story' (Conle, 2003, p12). The questions I have collected begin to surface here: how might narrative inquiry allow for 'differences within and among the stories of experience, how they are told and what it is that structures the telling and the retelling'; what is it 'that structures my own stories and my own intelligibility? What do my moral imperatives cost?' (Britzman, p 248). As a research methodology, narrative inquiry inevitably recognises the impossibility of telling everything, given both the partiality of language and the instability of meaning.

Clearly, if 'telling is partial and governed by the discourses of my time and place' (p 248), then in constructing narrative research, navigating time as a continuous process is fundamental. The concern is to avoid practices that undertake to complete or freeze narrative, and instead work against the grain of fixedness. Narrative inquirers must have tolerance for tentativeness and ambiguity, like artists, since narrative as a methodological approach is particular, contextual, relational and continuous. Barone (2001), too, suggests that our research ought to show a degree of textual ambiguity. The research text, like life, should be read as a continual unfolding in which the inquiry experiments with narrative forms to convey the sense that our storying is necessarily unfinished.

In narrative research, strategies to avoid freezing the research text might include establishing a response community or research conversations whilst developing an inquiry; generating field texts based on partnering journal writers; or evolving correspondences-letters exchanged between participants and researcher, for example, and other forms of collaborative research practices. Researchers can determine the shape and form of both field and research texts. In theatrical terms, our practices in process drama, improvisation, rehearsal or workshopping for new play development might be considered corresponding field text activities. Working with field and research texts (traditional or performative) as works-in-progress can encourage more sustained experimentation with form (research-as-improvisation/ performance).

Narrative inquiry suggests a methodological practice that is both process and product, and it is the relationship between these two elements that frames the application of narrative in my research and artmaking. Many of the questions opened by narrative discourses revolve around this reciprocal relationship. In translating narrative research terms through a drama education lens, our storied lives might be understood as pre-text (O'Neill, 1995). Private and public histories and memory reflected back into the stories we tell and remember, are told and re-told. In narrative inquiry, even the spaces between stories read or performed and the audience are not fixed but mediated by the narratives of our own lives. This methodology raises questions: how do we represent ourselves in the text and how do we find form for representing our storied lives in storied ways (Hatton, 2003)? Narrative inquiry can house the experiential nature of storied lives, and reflective work in drama education echoes this narrative dialogue in the documenting of our own and others' lives, within real or fictional contexts. In the story culture of drama education, we can move in or out of role, crossing from the present to inside the past, shifting both place and point of view (Zatzman, 2003).

Narrative methodologies provide a complementary route for researchers and artists to build theory and performance of our storied lives. In underlining the intersection(s) between narrative inquiry and drama education as research methodologies, the navigation of time – and the relationship between complex temporal boundaries – is a familiar and embodied strategy. Further, insofar as narrative inquiry is interested in exposing its own archeology of construction, I am inevitably brought to examine narrative through the authority of memory as it troubles temporal issues. Indeed, memory and meaning making in narrative inquiry practices collect and reflect back to, and with, communities their stories of identity.

Memory and Narrative Inquiry

Discourses about memory are complex and, like narrative inquiry itself, cross disciplinary boundaries. I offer conceptual approaches to questions of memory in order to support our engagement with narrative inquiry and the possibilities this methodology might open for research and art practices.

Retelling: memory and remembering are entirely implicated in narrative research in my translation of this methodology. If the telling of narratives is always about a 'second glance' (Britzman, 2003, p 246), then I am salted – Lot's Wife. By turning around (or drawing narratives forward), I confront the paradox of distance and intimacy in narrative, the tension of remembering and not remembering. This is, in essence, the fulcrum of the narrative project for my work. If memory is contextual and can be known only insofar as it is told, then narrative inquiry can be understood as a construction of the past, mediated and incomplete. Narrative inquiry moves out of the context of its own making, in which relationship is central to what narrative inquirers do, temporally and contextually (Clandinin and Connelly, 2000). I am intrigued by how narrative methodologies can generate and/or retrieve personal/collective memory; by the ways in which narrative inquiry can disrupt, question, or provide witness to pedagogical practices and understanding. Accordingly, much of my focus in narrative inquiry has been taken up by the shape of the memory-work I produce with students. For example, I have written elsewhere about the impetus to locate our own narratives and memory (personal, political and historical) specifically within the territory of Holocaust education, and acknowledge the lacuna that is the *Shoah* (Zatzman, 2003). The performance of memory, the obligation to witnessing, and representation(s) of narratives of identity have become critical to the designing of my arts education projects.

In his work on memory and memorial, James Young (2000, 1993) suggests that the most important 'space of memory' is 'not the space in the ground or above it but the space between the memorial and the viewer, between the viewer and his or her own memory: the place of the memorial in the viewer's mind, heart, and conscience' (2000, p 119). Bowell and Heap describe the space made available by process drama, in which the participants draw upon their life experiences, understanding that 'learners who gain a sense of ownership about their learning by having the opportunity to help shape its direction have a greater commitment to it and gain more from it as a result' (2001, p 46). Narrating lives in drama pedagogy means creating spaces for students to gather and re-assemble their own re-tellings, allowing young people to locate their lived experience in the interstices between histories, artmaking and narrative.

Re-telling: the revisioning of past experiences is produced as 'a powerful literary trope, part of the complex negotiations among memory, forgetting and ongoing interpretation that structure an examined life' (Suleiman, 1999, p 5). If our stories can be conceived as always available for re-telling, how might one interrogate forms of memory in narrative inquiry? I offer two shapes of memory, not mutually exclusive, with which to help navigate narrative research: post-memory and countermemory.

1. Post-memory

Hirsch (1997) distinguished 'post-memory from memory by generational distance and from history by deep personal connection'. Post-memory identifies the experience of 'those who grow up dominated by narratives that preceded their birth, whose own belated stories are displaced by the stories of the previous generations' (pp 22-23). While the notion of post-memory was borne within an after-Auschwitz ethos, its significance can be keenly felt in other communities for other histories. Hirsch has amplified the notion of post-memory over time, to contain the broader 'space of remembrance', a space in which if one can remember one's parents' memories, one can remember the suffering of others. As a narrative inquirer, I respond to Hirsch's account of post-memory's role in reflecting back on memory, revealing it as equally constructed and mediated by the dual processes of imagination and narration. Further, as a research methodology, narrative inquiry supports a range of forms for the surfacing of subtext so that in the performance of memory, the 'past is reinvented and textualised through the discourses and practices of the present' (Britzman, p 249).

Issues of post-memory can also be defined in terms of absence, insofar as narratives of invention replace recall for the second generation and beyond. Their narratives can only be mediated through the memories of others, because they themselves have no direct access to the past; for them, re-telling was either 'blocked by the radical disappearance of the older generation, or else by their traumatised silence' (Suleiman, 2003, p 6). Young also addresses issues of retelling and reception, in which he probes contemporary practices of memorial. Young describes how post-war artists explore both the necessity of memory and their incapacity to recall events never directly experienced (2000, pp6-9). This tension in re-telling is characteristic of much post-memory artmaking and affirms drama education's remarkable capacity to mediate amongst the fictional and the actual.

2. Countermemory

Countermemory stages the intersection of narrative and memory from a useful persepctive. Like post-memory, countermemory offers an approach to navigating narrative research. Artists who work with countermemory focus on creating anti-redemptory, self-conscious memorial spaces constructed specifically to challenge and resist the certainty of monumental forms. Contemporary memorial practices suggest that we must be awake to the possibility that finished monuments might actually negate the memory-work they were intended to honour, insofar as these memorials seem to represent and complete memory, doing the remembering for us. Indeed, Pierre Nora (1992) and Andreas Huyssen (2000) both caution that the more we build monuments, the less we remember. Instead, by conceptualising memory as unfinished, countermemorials are designed to represent the partial, unfixed, ephemeral composition of memory rather than providing 'definitive answers to impossible questions' (Young, 2000, p 2). Connelly and Clandinin's caution against fixing research texts in narrative inquiry is familiar here (2000). Countermemory hopes to engage the viewer in process, rather than allowing us to divest ourselves of the obligation to remember (Young, 2000, p 94).

Disappearing, invisible and other countermonuments can also help explicate narrative inquiry's approach to research in this architecture of retelling. By asking the viewer/audience/participant to look back to his/her own memory, countermemory opens a narrative space for every new generation to find their own significance in the past or present. Just as narrative research might address the tension of theorising lived experience as discontinuous and chaotic rather than seamless and orderly (Britzman, 2003, p 249), countermonuments stress 'the provocation of uncertainty, anxiety, and self-interrogation as matters of design' (Rosenberg, 2000, p 84). By defining themselves in opposition to a traditional memorial's task and conventions, countermemorials aim:

> not to console but to provoke; not to remain fixed but to change; not to be everlasting but to disappear; not to be ignored by passersby but to demand interaction; not to remain pristine but to invite its own violation and desanctification; not to accept graciously the burden of memory but to throw it back at [their] feet (Young, 1993, p 30).

Countermemory's pedagogical and aesthetic undertaking provides compelling possibilities for shaping narrative in arts education practices, particularly since the three dimensional space of narrative methodology deliberately examines our storied lives in terms of place, lived experience and the temporal. In the IDIERI narrative research station, several countermemorials were referenced, projects which deliberately left no trace of the memorial act. These installations were designed as interventions into public space, acknowledging the rupture between what is absent and how we might recall and represent it.

My own work in drama education and narrative has been shaped by these discourses and I have developed fine arts practices that invite students to write themselves into their and others' generational stories and to explore the possibility of *creating* memory. Central to my practice is the recognition that what we choose to tell, to whom and how, all matter (Zatzman, 2003, p 36). As both a temporal and imaginative journey, narrative inquiry offers young people the opportunity to trace history 'both remembered and not remembered, transmitted and not transmitted' (Horowitz, 1998, p 278). Through narrative inquiry, youth can theorise their lives in performance as acts of retrieval. Focusing upon the conceptual nature of memory, working through and against competing stories and the narration of experience, narrative inquiry pushes at the boundaries of my practice, not only by questioning how to tell our stories and to whom, but also by suggesting complex temporal frames, in which our narratives are constructed at least twice: once from the 'then-perspective' of the original context of the story, and layered again in the 'now-perspective' at the time of (re-) telling (Conle, 1999).

Art Speigelman's *Maus* (1996) provides an example of the complex construction of artmaking, narrative and memory that illuminates much of my theorising around narrative inquiry. *Maus* presents an (apparently) subversive use of cartoon to depict the Holocaust, in which all the Jewish characters are represented as mice, all the Germans as cats (Nazi propaganda and the Final Solution are clearly referenced). The *Maus* narrative functions on at least three levels of inquiry. *Maus* tells the story of the Holocaust: a) through the voice of Speigelman's father, Vladek, a survivor of Auschwitz; b) through the narration of the father's experience to Artie, his artist son; c) through Spiegelman's reflexive work in witnessing and retelling his father's story as he struggles to shape (what we must now understand to be) *their* story. In this visual narrative, there is no single linear or chrono-logical thread moving the story in time and place. Maus utterly inter-rupts the temporal logic of traditional past/present, or before, during and after the Holocaust. Spiegelman narrates from the site of the pre-sent, from which he writes and draws, exposing moments of com-plexity and contradiction. The temporal levels sometimes seem to blur or collapse into one another. 'Vladek's story does not remain a narrative of a concluded past, an experience that is dead and buried; rather, it is perceived as contemporaneous reality, a part of Art's life that cannot be relegated to the past tense' (McGlothlin, 2003, p 194).

Artie – the son who listens to his father's stories, is further distin-guished from Art – the second-generation artist who struggles, para-doxically, with his inability to represent the story in visual terms. The narrative act occurs with the integration of the father's trauma into the son's memory through the very agency of narrative, the act of (re) telling (p 180-2). In *Maus,* memory and narrative produce the story of the father and son's struggle to live with – or their inability to live with – each other and this painful legacy (Levin, 1997). Demonstrating elements of both post and countermemory, *Maus* locates us inside the 'multiple aspects of both time and narrative function – the past of the Holocaust story, the present time of memory and discourse, and the timeless moment of narrating' (McGlothlin, 2003, p194). We are witness to the comic book's shifting representations of past and present, artist and father, and art-making itself.

Maus highlights another important feature of narrative inquiry as a research methodology: insofar as we are not alone in this space that enfolds us and those with whom we work, narrative inquiry is a relational inquiry. My narrative is located by placing myself 'in the midst of a nested set of stories, ours and theirs' (Clandinin and Connelly, 2000, p 63). As inquirers in narrative, we meet ourselves in the past, the present and the future. Telling stories of ourselves in the past leads to the possibility of retellings. Moreover, it is not only the participants' stories that are retold by a narrative inquirer; it might also be the inquirers' stories that are open for inquiry and retelling. This is significant given that we are complicit in the world we study. Working within a three-dimensional narrative inquiry space means that as researchers we become visible within our own lived and told stories (pp 60-62).

Narrative inquiry may not only reference individual storied lives but, as a methodology, it may signal a focus on narratives of place or geography. The memory of place and issues of absence might also be constructed as constituents of a narrative inquiry. For example, in the powerful space of absence, Daniel Libeskind's Jewish Museum in Berlin stands as an evocation of the erasure and void of Berlin's Jewish life. This museum site was designed so that 'to cross from one museum-space to the other, the visitors traverse sixty bridges opening into the Void-space: the embodiment of absence' (Libeskind, 1998). Numerous IDIERI events – workshops, research conversations, performances – provided opportunities to improvise within the space of absence. Indeed, notions of absence came to provide one of the conceptual frames that our narrative research station examined. Narrative inquiry provided a methodological stance from which to begin to shape our stories of diaspora, personal and public memories of absence and dislocation, as expressions of identity and place within drama and theatre processes.

Finally, the work of post-memory artists is compelling because, as a narrative inquirer looking backward to draw stories forward, I wear the skin of memory, bound as I am to devising a culture of story. David Booth has long advocated the power and need for story in our lives (1994). Booth outlines the process of building a story culture, encouraging teachers to understand the possibilities of story (1999, p3). Narrative inquiry supports a story culture by offering possibilities for critically examining our narratives, performing identity and provoking story communities.

How does narrative inquiry aid an understanding of practice?

Reflections on narrative practice borne of and during the IDIERI conference were not restricted to stories of the daily drama workshops we all attended. Rather, formal research conversations, and informal breakfast conversations; performances; paper presentations and chats over coffee all constituted pieces of the research landscape. Premised on the researcher's own narrative of experience, narrative inquiry bleeds into autobiography and shares many disciplinary boundaries with life writing/autoethnography. As narrative inquirers we asked 'questions of who we are in the field and who we are in the texts that we write on our experience of the field experience' (Clandinin and Connelly, 2000, p 70). Questions to extend understanding of narrative. Questions themselves become a record of practice:

> *Where do you connect to the work of the IDIERI drama workshops? What is resonant in the research conversations to which you are witness? In performances? In papers sessions? Everything counts. Start documenting. Recording. Construct/ assemble field texts from all you see. Collect ephemera: your RSC Richard III ticket with notes written in the dark of the theatre; a piece of University College Northampton stationery on which is scrawled the record of an unexpected conversation about housing youth theatre projects within strategic places that speak to the history of a community; even the train ticket to Northampton holds the journey. Each piece fragile, fleeting evidence of breath, of memory; field texts all.*

In narrative inquiry, field texts are understood as fundamental to the retrieval of memory and the shaping of inquiry. Field texts might be translated as 'a constructed sequence of time, the liminal space between an event and recall, the memory of memory' (Sleziak, 2000). Examples of field texts might also include photographs, which attempt to capture experiences through 'images that inform/re-form re/search' (Grauer, *et al*, 2000) or journals. Journals – a familiar reflective tool in drama pedagogy – can hold detailed records about the existential conditions of place, time, events, images, inner monologues, questions – all narrative expressions of inquiry. A detailed recording of field notes might later allow the researcher to excavate memory, to spend time inside another's stories and re-tell that research landscape, even months or years later.

In the narrative inquiry research station, we kept field notes of our ongoing conversations for each day of the conference on large sheets of flip paper. What remains inscribed on those papers are constructed representations of experience: forms of those textualised identities (Britzman, 2000). While an essential part of the inquiry process, field texts may or may not become part of the final research product. Field notes might be understood as a workshop rendering of a play, which is later edited and reshaped to produce the performance or research text. Now, from the present, fragments of my and the IDIERI participants' field and research texts break the surface of this inquiry. Questions embedded in these texts provide a sense of the critical and material constructions with which one might begin to structure a narrative inquiry.

field notes/research text 1

Fragments of conversations about/in narrative inquiry:

How do we gather 'texts' for our research?

What does the process of revisiting these texts over time reveal to us as researchers using a narrative inquiry approach?

How do we explore and/or resolve issues of: ethics, politics/ ideologies, theories embedded within the narrative research? (frames)

What methods do we use to make sense of layers of meaning operating within the narratives we use/create?

How do we manage narrative inquiry as a temporal construct?

How do we manage contradictory narratives in the drama and research processes

in our role as – witness, recorder, interpreter of others' lived stories, narrator, educator? (resonance)

What does the research text look like? (form, audience)

field notes/research text 2

Texts: sketches paintings photographs sculpture performance video sound

Texts: autobiography/ biography/ memoir/ email/ letters

Texts: are you writing without end (diary)? or writing against the end (journal)?

Texts: record of movement(s), record of gender in the inquiry

Texts: as ontologies (becoming vs. being); temporal texts

How does archive become research text(s)/ performance(s)?

How do we respond to the challenge of creating 'texts' that are not disconnected from the inquiry experience?

What is the throughline that reaches across my field texts and into the re-search text, situating my experiences within the three dimensional narrative inquiry space?

How do we create research texts that acknowledge memory and its place in our narrative inquiry? How do we create form for memory that is selective, shaped, and retold in the continuum of my experiences?

How do we avoid factual, unnuanced representations of memory in the research text?
Have you considered field texts as memory signposts of experience? Triggered memory?
Have you re-visoned ephemera as traces of a life? As research texts?
How is your sense of history and memory based upon intertextual links made among narratives?

In offering the opportunity to navigate narrative as a research methodology, even this chapter should have been, had time allowed, a conversation in text, passed back and forth between me and the participants in the narrative inquiry station. Together, we could have laboured over the process and form of this telling – a kind of post-card; later, our correspondence to Jonothan Neelands and his players postcards to mark place and experience in Northampton.

field notes 3/postcards from Northampton

▨ *We collected ephemera during our time here in Northampton. Those little slips of coloured paper that were the tickets to each of the activities, for example. Doorways into memory. I hold one of them in my hand and am there again when Dorothy Heathcote wept. I saw her remembering her husband at the kitchen table. What is the significance of memory? we are asking in this research. My narrative as a young teacher juxtaposed against the memories of this splendid old woman. But maybe there's some hope for me – I could sense her man's presence at/absence from the chair at the table they recreated for us in their IDIERI conversation. When Dorothy and Gavin spoke and remembered her husband, I was sitting with them for a moment, at the kitchen table, somewhere else in England in another time.*

▨ *Time is collapsed when I pull out my train ticket. I am back at the IDIERI conference so many months ago. I am back in the room. Jane danced ethnography as performance here. In real time. In looped time. In remembered time, I am back in that large room; it's early still, cool grey morning light. The large wooden floor at the centre is empty with the anticipation of moving back into our stories. I am back inside Pedro's story, inside Jane's dance, inside my struggle to be a better teacher.*

■ *I wonder about the authority of Neelands' directions, the authority of gender in the scenes, and questioned the authority of my own narrative. Can I actually create a research document built on my own stories? Do I need more quantitative/academic structures? I am questioning everything now. Belarie says even my questions have a place here.*

■ *My head is swimming with methodological frames for looking at the data. On this side of me I see one group charting every movement; the other group is recording gender. We are looking for resonant images and texts. I didn't know there were so many ways to look.*

■ *Narrative inquiry: ... the experiences of abandonment and restoration to grace through reflection and sharing of the narrative of abandonment ... I mentioned as abandonments the act of decision involved in choosing places for meals at IDIERI, the visit to Stratford, waiting for the bus that separated us off from the rest of the party, walking around Stratford alone in the rain, the children and adult relatives abandoned to their fate in* Richard III, *the abandoned characters who featured in Jonothan's lessons, like Polynices, and Antigone's determination to honour him, to be herself abandoned, and the healing effect of reflection and sharing through narrative.*

When Neelands spoke with representatives of each IDIERI research station, he explained that because the story at the centre of each of his lessons is known, his drama work must necessarily move around inside the existing frame of the narrative. The boundaries of the story cannot be changed; the large narrative is laid out. But I suggest that while all choices may already be made within the story, narrative inquiry as a complementary methodology for drama research allows for the possibility of extending our relationship to the narrative structure. Rather than considering the stories' structures as one of Neelands' 'necessary constraints', it could be that narrative inquiry provides one of his 'necessary freedoms' in allowing us to enter the ruptures between the existing episodic text and texts of personal history and memory. That I locate myself within those cracks reflects a practice informed by post-memory discourses. Narrative inquiry's impulse to mediate between our personal stories and narratives embedded in a performance, text or image may also be understood as a blueprint from the theatre that we recognise – the contextual nature of performance. For example, theatre designed to create an en-counter between the text(s) of a play and the public and private narratives of its audience is evidenced by Susan Sontag's 1993 staging of Act I of *Waiting for Godot* in war-torn Sarajevo (Sontag, 1994). Or in drama education, the *Looking for Shakespeare* programme mediated between young people's own narratives and their engage-ment with Shakespeare (Martin-Smith, 2000). Hatton's devised theatre work excavates girls' knowledge and experience, foreground-ing their need to tell and stage their own storied lives. Her research highlights agency not only in the telling of their own narratives, but in witnessing and enabling the staging of their co-creators (2003).

To understand the mediation between our storied lives and the texts we encounter in narrative practices better, I reference one source Neelands drew upon at IDIERI, a picture book entitled *the composition* (Skármeta and Ruano, 1998). Neelands brilliantly edged us into the story of Pedro, a boy in grade three, full of life, sensitive to the everyday whirling about him, a kid who would occupy every moment with soccer if he could. To the ordinary, the narrative brings the extraordinary: the confrontation with a dictatorship that Pedro struggles to understand. Between the small delights of childhood (playing soccer with his friends, scoring goals, dreaming of owning a leather soccer ball like real soccer players use, dinners with his mother and father), we discover the impact of the dictatorship within Pedro's small community:

> *'Goal!' screamed Pedro. He waited for his friend's applause. But no one was paying any attention. Everyone was staring at Don Daniel's grocery store... Daniel's father was being dragged down the street by two men. A group of soldiers were pointing machine guns at him. When Daniel tried to approach his father, a soldier pushed him back.*
> *'Calm down,' said the soldier.*
> *Don Daniel looked at his son. 'take care of the store for me,' he said.*
> *As the soldiers pushed him toward a jeep, Don Daniel tried to put his hand in his pocket. Immediately a soldier raised his machine gun.*
> *'Careful!' he shouted.*
> *'I want to give my son the keys to the store,' Don Daniel said.*

Neelands introduced us to the landscape of this narrative so that by degrees, through the eyes of his parents, the teacher, the children in his town and Pedro himself, we become witness to the events and consequences of this world. How do I excavate this story? From a narrative inquiry stance, I shared with my colleagues my own re-inscribing of *the composition*, to which I bring forward narratives of resistance, located as I am within fine arts and Holocaust research. Post-memory: how do I move through a temporal and imaginative inquiry, tracing a history both transmitted and not transmitted, remembered and not remembered, in this source which serves as pretext for our drama work? What kind of agency is there in the act of narrating? In what ways is not telling/not remembering an erasure, a dissolution of identity in the story of Pedro? Can we create a research text in response to *the composition*, about the process of erasure or the absence of presence? What might that text look like? What moments will you re-tell and why? Whose story is it? Initially, I suggested that the IDIERI participants look for powerful images or texts while observing Neelands' work. Which images or texts in the master classes are resonant? How do each of us enter the text? Later, when we move more deeply into issues of memory and memorial, we will interrogate notions of witness (manifest on so many levels across IDIERI) and the obligation to testimony in framing this work. Again, I am reminded that narrative inquiry, like drama education, is both process and product; we are witness to and participant in our storied lives here in Northampton and later, at home when we continue to reflect on our practices.

field notes 4/Witness

■ *Yesterday Jonothan started with a letter. It was the story of a boy. Today we watched him establish the 3D space of Pedro's classroom. If text in narrative inquiry can be a photo, letter, scenes or visual arts, then can classroom walls be text too? When we watched the session today, the strongest images for me were when they improvised what might be hidden in Pedro's classroom, working against the dictatorship. Even as observers we were in on the secret, really, because we knew how their underground resistance was created. It was exhilarating. What things are hidden in my classroom?*

■ *Pedro is so hot for me. I am horrified at being inextricably drawn into that world. I see the danger coming. I recognise it. I know people whose names were put on a list. There is no redemption. Stop the telling. Tell the children to run.*

■ *A theme that kept recurring in the drama sessions context as well as in some of the paper sessions was the notion of witness or by-*

stander. During the drama practice we were exposed to content that included witnesses of crime and at the same time we (on the outer circle) were witnessing their working process. In many ways we were bystanders, unable to influence the process. Like many of the scenarios worked in the sessions, we felt powerless to shape the class. I am not suggesting this was a bad thing. It is simply an observation. This feeling helped me re-evaluate my teaching. I want to ensure that I create a learning environment where we witness content or stories, yet the bystanders (students) have the opportunity to change the situation. I need to create space for students to influence the outcome. I also need to provide them with ways or tools that enable them to create that change. I need to find ways to empower the witness, to fight against impotence. What are the seeds I can plant? How can I then fertilise to maximise growth and learning? My objective is not for them to learn my way of teaching or approaching the subject, but for them to discover their way, their strength, their approach into the content...

What does it mean to witness something not actually experienced? I pose this question both from inside and outside this narrative context(s). We, in the research stations, sat as witness/bystander watching Pedro's story and others'. Neelands carried us into the Pedro narrative so that while I was sitting low to the ground on the long wooden benches in Northampton, I was huddled beside that green radio in Pedro's living room, listening with them in secret. Mediated by imagination and memory, I could leap into the stories Neelands and his students were re-telling. As witnesses to the master classes, we are at once both contained by the narrative and voyeur. Do we bring our teaching stories to Jonothan's teaching; and, where are we in your stories, Jonothan? When I asked participants to place themselves at the centre of their examination of Neelands' work, it is because of the need to interrogate our critical locatedness within the inquiry. Narrative inquiry can situate 'staged conversation(s)' so that collaborative processes in drama can dynamically recall lived experiences (van Manen, 1997) and invite meaning-making as students' stories are staged in action (Hatton, 2003, p 42).

For at least one of the participants in the research station, the subjectivities of this stance and the transparency of this subjectivity was problematic-as she searched for 'objective' research, despite our caution that in a contemporary research paradigm, an idealised, normalising objectivity may not exist. The limitation of engaging in narrative inquiry at IDIERI *vis a vis* time constraints is also noted. In narrative inquiry, what one is exploring and finds puzzling changes as the research progresses; as narratives are retold, puzzles shift, and purposes change over time (Clandinin and Connelly, 2000, p 73). This fluidity in the process of researching our storied lives accounts for some of the frustration in coming to grips with ambiguity, the provisional, or the contradictory uncertainties in the doing of the inquiry. It is challenging to recognise significant moments in our own stories, even without the constraint of durational issues. How does one recognise which stories to draw forward or which narratives are or will be resonant? The examination of sets of narrative statements over time can help distinguish narrative processes of change (Conle, 2003, p 12) and can situate our acts of teaching as they are uncovered within the experience of everyday life (Grumet, 1991).

field notes 5/ Every moment is two moments...

◼ *Learning about Narrative Inquiry research at the IDIERI Conference has led me on an unexpected journey. I did not know what narrative inquiry was and felt surprised that participating in this method of research would require me to explore my own narrative. I have always been a reflective person, yet when it came to determining a single moment I could recall that would link with the dominating issues of the research for the week, I had to dig deeply through the layers of memories and defining moments within my realm of experience. Luckily I had people around me willing to listen to me and to offer suggestions on how to discover this defining moment. And one day of teaching can provide dozens of defining moments if we look hard enough.*

◼ *My task was to formulate questions and choose text from the practice sessions we were watching. I was reminded by Belarie of the necessity to place myself in the centre of my question; why was I asking these particular questions? Most importantly, how would the responses or research into them help me move forward with the research to become a better educator and drama practitioner? By the end of the practice sessions, the dominating theme and text that stood out for me as a narrative inquirer was the theme of what seems to be humans' desire to isolate and create distance from a problem.*

When I finally return to Toronto and my own IDIERI field notes, I wander through *the composition* (which, curiously, I stumbled upon unexpectedly in a downtown bookstore), and find myself carrying forward my own post-memories. Faced with the story of Pedro in Northampton, I wondered about resistance, about whether we will have to listen to the radio in secret, again, and the choices we make and the questions we confront in light of that history. As an artist/ educator, I recognise that in gathering and staging stories —retelling the past and reshaping myself in the present – the act of narrating takes up the challenge of finding form for questions and aesthetics in the performance or representation of research. My own history and memory lives in tandem with the stories in our classrooms and communities even if unfinished and contradictory: 'Every moment is two moments' (Michaels, 1996, p 140). Inevitably, I draw this doubleness into the aesthetic space of my drama classroom, self-consciously and critically allowing these 'two moments' to illuminate my curricular choices in form and process.

Drama pedagogy and narrative inquiry can hold diverse identity locations (Grady, 2000), positioning my stories of survival, Pedro's and yours. These methodologies support the 'capacity to know/ narrate' our own stories (Gallagher, 2003 p 11). Further, as a narrative inquirer working within an aesthetic frame, even the page on which this text is written can be understood as part of my telling, a space for palimpsests of experience. How might the page be inscribed by memory and narrative? Can fragments of this text be printed on vellum so that we might discern layers of lived experience through opaque transparency? Can we envision language as script, both typed and handwritten for differing narratives, sites, times? Even this page is visual text and not outside the story of narrative inquiry. You are not simply reading but scripted into the act of witness and retrieval.

Other possibilities for narrative inquiry

Everyone in teacher education needs the space and encouragement to raise questions that attend to the possible and acknowledge the uncertainty of our educational lives. For in doing so, we can begin to envision the discourses, voices, and discursive practices that can invite the possible. (Britzman, 2003, p 241)

After Britzman, I invite you to question your interpretative glance. Questioning: in embodying other possibilities for narrative inquiry, I turn to face the questions I have been excavating throughout. Questions as narrative, as memory-work. Questions, framed as both process and product. Questions now subsume this narrative and structure the inquiry. Now these questions stand as a provocation to interrogate your texts and responses; an invitation to grapple with shaping a narrative inquiry for your own research.

How do our stories live on within us?

How do our stories live on in other, more recent stories?

When or where are history and (auto)biography joined in my inquiry?

What constraints are placed on an individual's ability to narrate a self?

Which narratives intersect in the work for you?

How can narrative inquiry help negotiate among collaborators in creating a response community?

Have you returned to your research community, to ask not 'Have I got it right? Is this what you said/ what you do?' but rather to inquire about broader questions of identity: 'Is this you? Do you see yourself here'? (Clandinin and Connelly, 2000)

How should our stories be transcribed, recorded, circulated to help develop a shared narrative inquiry or ethnographic authority?

How do we represent ourselves in the text?

How should I translate storied field texts into research texts?

How should our stories be transcribed, recorded and circulated to create art, to perform research?

How can a narrative inquiry methodology translate into my art making?

In what ways does narrative inquiry allow for collaboration in my artmaking?

How do we represent temporal issues in arts-based research? Visually? In performance?

Can I make manifest my post-memory relationships in the research/ performance I produce?

How can texts, images, ephemera organise memory?

How do we include voices heard and not heard?

Can we address the silences we choose and those of which we are unaware?

Who's present in the story?

Who's absent?

Can we embody the places of rupture in our inquiry?

How do we avoid freezing narrative?

How does narrative inquiry as research help us respond to what we've heard? to locate subjectivies?

What importance do these stories have on my development as a teacher? On my arts practice?

In conceiving other possibilities for narrative inquiry, I look to artists who explore storied landscapes and the boundaries among text, image and context; artists who improvise with forms and tropes of self-portraiture and lay bare the promise in writing multiple texts of their storied lives. I am conscious of distinguishing how a range of artistic texts are constructed, represented and narrated, given that each variation on narrative practice makes the world visible in a different way. I am hungry to examine and make manifest my own narrative questions in the very forms of inquiry I encounter and create, as I work to narrate an evolving sense of memory and identity in research/artistic practices. Accordingly, as a methodology for constructing and performing meaning, I commend narrative inquiry to you as a possible world.

Recommended Reading

Britzman, Deborah (2003) *Practice Makes Practice: A Critical Study of Learning to Teach.* Revised edition. New York, SUNY

Clandinin, D. Jean and F. Michael Connelly (2000). *Narrative Inquiry: Experience and Story in Qualitative Research.* San Francisco, Jossey-Bass Inc.

Conle, Carola (2003) 'An Anatomy of Narrative Curricula' in *Educational Researcher,* April 32(3), pp 3-15

Hatton, Chris. (2003) 'Backyards and Borderlands: Some Reflections on Researching the Travels of Adolescent Girls Doing Drama' in *Drama Australia Journal,* NJ, 27(1)

Zatzman, Belarie (2003) 'The Monologue Project: Drama as a Form of Witnessing' in Booth, D. and Gallagher, K. eds *How Theatre Educates: Convergences and Counterpoints with Artists, Scholars, and Advocates.* Toronto, University of Toronto Press

References

Barone, T., (2001) *Touching eternity: The enduring outcomes of teaching.* New York, Teachers College Press

Booth, David ed. (1999) 'Story Matters: The Role of Story in School' in *Orbit* 30 (3)

Booth, David (1994) *Story drama.* Markham: Pembroke Publishers

Bowell, P. and Heap, B.S. (2001) *Planning Process Drama.* London, David Fulton

Britzman, Deborah (2003) *Practice Makes Practice: A Critical Study of Learning to Teach.* Revised edition, New York, SUNY

Clandinin, D. Jean and F. Michael Connelly (2000) *Narrative Inquiry: Experience and Story in Qualitative Research.* San Francisco, Jossey-Bass Publishers

Conle, Carola (2003) 'An Anatomy of Narrative Curricula' in *Educational Researcher*, April 32(3), pp 3-15

Conle, Carola. (1999). Why narrative? Which narrative? Struggling with time and place in life and research in *Curriculum Inquiry* (1). 7-31

Gallagher, Kathleen. (2003) 'Emergent Cnceptions in Theatre Pedagogy and Production' in Booth, D. and Gallagher, K. eds *How Theatre Educates: Convergences and Counterpoints with Artists, Scholars, and Advocates*. Toronto, University of Toronto Press

Grady, Sharon (2000). *Drama and Diversity*. Portsmouth: Heinemann

Grauer, Kit, Irwin Rita L., de Cosson, Alex, Wilson, Sylvia. (2001) 'Images for Understanding: Snapshots of Learning through the Arts' in *International Journal of Education and the Arts*, http://ijea.asu.edu/v2n9/

Grumet, M. (1991) 'Curriculum and the Art of Daily Life.' In *Reflections from the Heart of Educational Inquiry: Understanding Curriculum and Teaching through the Arts*. State University of New York Press

Hatton, Chris. (2003) 'Backyards and Borderlands: Some Reflections on Researching the Travels of Adolescent Girls Doing Drama' in *Drama Australia Journal*, NJ, 27(1)

Hirsch, Marianne. (1997) *Family Frames: Photography, Narrative and Postmemory*. Cambridge, Harvard University Press

Hirsch, Marianne. (2001) 'Surviving Images: Holocaust Photographs and the Work of Postmemory' *The Yale Journal of Criticism* 14(1), Spring 2001 pp 5-37, New Haven, Yale University and Johns Hopkins University Press

Horowitz, Sara (1998) 'Auto/Biography and Fiction After Auschwitz' in Efraim Sicher, (ed.) *Breaking Crystal: Writing and Memory after Auschwitz*. University of Illinois Press, 1998

Huysen, Andreas, (2000) 'Present Pasts: Media, Politics, Amnesia,' *Public Culture*, 12.1, pp 21-38

Knowles, J. G. and Thomas, S. (2001). 'Insights and Inspiration from an Artist's Work, Envisioning and Portraying Lives in Context' in Cole, A.L. and Knowles, J.G., eds Lives in *Context: the Art of Life History Research*. Walnut Creek, AltaMira Press

Levin, M. (1997) *Maus* in *Globe* and *Mail*, 15 February 1997, Arts: D10

Libeskind, Daniel (1998) *Between the Lines: The Jewish Museum Berlin*. http://www.jmberlin.de/pdf_en/between_the_lines.pdf

Martin-Smith, Alistair 'Looking for Shakespeare: Role-playing within the role,' *Drama Research: The Research Journal of National Drama*, Volume 1, April 2000, pp 93-107

Michaels, Anne (1996) *Fugitive Pieces*. Toronto, McClelland and Stewart

McGlothlin, E. (2003) 'No Time Like the Present: Narrative and Time in Art Spiegelman's *Maus*' in *Narrative*, 11(2) May 2003 Columbus, Ohio State University

Nora, Pierre, ed (1992) *Realms of Memory: Rethinking the French Past*, Columbia University Press

O'Neill, Cecily (1995) *Drama Worlds: A Framework for Process Drama*. Portsmouth, Heinemann

Rosenberg, Sharon (2000) 'Standing in a Circle of Stone: Rupturing the Binds of Emblematic Memory' in Roger I. Simon, Sharon Rosenberg and Claudia Eppert, (eds.) *Between Hope and Despair: Pedagogy and the Remembrance of Historical Trauma*, Lantham, Rowman and Littlefield

Sicher, Efraim, ed (1998) *Breaking Crystal: Writing and Memory after Auschwitz.* University of Illinois Press

Skármeta, Antonio and Ruano, Alfonso (1998) *the composition.* Toronto, Groundwood Books

Sleziak, Zofia (2000) *Liminal Spaces within a Contemporary Australian Arts Practice. Abstract Stagings of Fleeting Narratives: Alluding to Memory.* http://www.brunel.ac.uk/depts/pfa/bstjournal/1no1/ZOFIASLEZIAK.html

Sontag, Susan (1994) '*Waiting for Godot* in Sarajevo' in *Performing Arts Journal*, 16 (2)

Spiegelman, A. (1996) *The Complete Maus.* NY, Pantheon

Suleiman, S.R. and Hirsch, M. (2003) 'Material Memory: Holocaust Testimony in Post-Holocaust Art' in Hornstein, S. and Jacobowitz, F. eds *Image and Remembrance: Representation of the Holocaust.* Indiana University Press

Suleiman, Susan Rubin. (Summer 1999) 'Reflections on Memory at the Millennium'. 1999 Presidential Address http://www.geocities.com/resistancehistory/article06.html

van Manen, M. (1997) *Researching Lived Experience: Human Science for an Action Sensitive Pedagogy.* Second edition, London, Ontario, Althouse Press

Young, James E. (2000) *At Memory's Edge: After-Images of the Holocaust in Contemporary Art and Architecture.* Yale University Press

Young, James E. (1993) *The Texture of Memory: Holocaust Memorials and Meaning.* Yale University Press

Zatzman, Belarie (2005) 'Staging History: Aesthetics and the Performance of Memory' in Special Issue on the Aesthetics of Drama and Theatre in Education in *The Journal of Aesthetic Education*, Volume 39, Number 2, pp. 1-10 (in press).

Zatzman, Belarie (2003) 'The Monologue Project: Drama as a Form of Witnessing' in Booth, D. and Gallagher, K. eds *How Theatre Educates: Convergences and Counterpoints with Artists, Scholars, and Advocates.* University of Toronto Press

7

The Feeling of the Experience: a methodology for performance ethnography

Jane Bacon

An introduction to performance ethnography

This chapter is about performance ethnography and its particular accumulation of processes which comprise the methodological approach. It has been developed from dance anthropologists and ethnographers, performance practitioners and performance studies, and is applied here to the specific context of applied arts. The primary premise of an ethnographic approach is the study of a group of people. In this instance I am developing a particular methodological approach called performance ethnography that aims to value the *experience* of both researcher and researched within a creative environment such as the applied arts. This methodology relies on the researcher's ability to be attuned to the potential of experiential knowledge that arises when working through a reflexive approach. In this way the researcher should be working toward an embodied understanding, or the feeling of the experience, of the creative aspects that are specific to the research context. This embodied knowledge, or embodied reflexive practice, should provide the ground upon which the ethnographic data can then best be represented.

Performance ethnography, as I describe it here, was applied by a group of researchers during IDIERI. Twelve delegates chose to participate in a research station on performance ethnography and this chapter uses their experiences as its basis. The researchers carefully studied a group of students participating in a drama education workshop. The tasks set for those researchers and the tasks set for you in the chapter (which can be found in the text boxes) are specific tools and methods that aim to develop your ability to seek meaning in the research through the experiential. This is a creative embodied engagement with the subject of study that aims to assist the researcher in her ability to speak from experience, in an attempt to find a common language of experience where both researcher and researched might speak about creative work.

As a dance ethnographer and a performer I have developed this methodological approach in the study of particular groups of people (Bacon, 2003), which is the essence of ethnography, and in the making of my own interdisciplinary and multi-media performance work, or practice as research, as it has become known in academic circles in the United Kingdom. This isn't a semiotic analysis of an objective text and it isn't a phenomenological approach to the analysis of performance. It doesn't exclude or preclude the use of theories from other areas, such as those outlined in other chapters in this book. The key concern is assisting those involved in research in the applied arts to discover a language that can speak from, through and with the body. When both researcher and researched can begin to engage with the creative work in its own right then the discussion that emanates from that practical engagement may generate its own very particular theoretical concerns.

Performance ethnography is not a new concept. Yordon (1997) suggests that an ethnographic approach to theatre-making would mean selecting a group of people or cultural group to study and then create performance material from these experiences or assist the participants to make work for and about themselves. Whilst this method of generating a stimulus for the creation of performance might be an interesting approach, it is an outdated approach and a potential colonising of the 'other', or subject of study, and as such, represents much of what has been deemed problematic within the discipline of anthropology in the last century (Fox, 1991, Bacon, 2005). Such a creative process would need careful ethical consideration.

My reasons for mentioning Yordon is that this example is an artistic one within a social scientific framework, even though the rationale for applying ethnographic methods to theatre-making are not congruent with my own construction of performance ethnography. Whilst the need for well-researched evidence in the applied arts is crucial, we need to be wary of the usurpation of methodologies from other disciplines without due consideration to the context within which these methods will be employed. A creative context may have its own particular demands that require the researcher to think beyond traditional ethnographic methodologies. The process of data selection in Yordon's example, and in ethnographic approaches more generally, could be considered to be an artistic one, similar to the making of performance or the teaching of drama, music, dance or performing arts (Woolcot, 1995, Willis, 2000). The approach outlined here *could* result in the possibility of 'making' performance from and with the participants but that is not the key thrust of this work. Perhaps this is better understood as a processual approach rather than product-orientated in that this chapter is not concerned with the subsequent representation of the subject of study but with the methodological approach that leads the researcher to a particular representation. The methodology is the rationale for the selection of particular methods or tools that can then be applied in the gathering of data.

Before moving on to more detailed exploration of performance ethnography the terminology in this chapter needs to be explained. When I refer to 'participants', I mean the people who participated in the drama workshops at IDIERI. In your own research your participants are the subject of your study. The 'researchers' are those who participated in the 'research station'. By 'fieldsite' I mean the 'area' of study which might be geographically defined or it might more clearly relate to your 'subject of study' and therefore be defined by the group of people themselves.

Throughout the chapter you will find tasks to use in your research environment to practically engage with both the creative tools and the reflexive approach of the methodology. In order to do these tasks you don't have to be doing fieldwork at this present moment but you do need to be able to try these tasks out practically. You might do this in other environments, such as teaching or leading workshops, as they are suitable for numerous situations. You will also need to devote time to creative contemplation of your real or imagined field-site. The examples in the text boxes are generic and can be altered to fit your fieldsite. They are not intended to be a comprehensive guide to performance ethnography but are included to assist your understanding of an embodied reflexive practice.

Developing an embodied reflexive practice

The activities the researcher can access or in which she can participate, the techniques chosen and the relationship between these techniques, are based on an assumption that the personal relationships established between researcher and researched are the primary medium for obtaining information (Amit, 2000, p 2). The nature of this information, or material, cannot or should not be pre-determined as the role of the researcher is to come to the work aware of her own expectations (reflexivity) in order to explore the field freely and openly. Reflexivity is a sociological activity which requires the researcher to 'think about one's commitment critically and responsibly' in order to understand the relation between the researcher and the creation of knowledge (Varela, 1995, p 71). Probyn (1993) suggests that self-reflexivity is a global term often used to describe many different things from 'a metatheoretical reflection upon the activity of writing texts' to the naming of 'a phenomenological or experiential moment of interacting with others in the field' (1993, p 62).

In this research, developing an embodied reflexive approach is a tool that will bring clarity to the author-informant relationships and illuminate the appropriateness of decisions made concerning the representations of informants. It may also help to locate the reader in relation to the author because the role of the author is explicit rather than implicit, thereby allowing the reader to decide whether or not to agree with the author. In other words 'I tell you *how* I have come to know what I know so that you can make up your own mind' (Stanley and Wise, 1990). In this sense the researchers in the applied arts environment are interpretive researchers who may usefully think of themselves as an ethnographer as doing so will give a particular viewpoint or set of tools for the analysis of the fieldsite or research setting. Through this embodied reflexive practice the researcher is able to examine and explicate the nature of the interaction with the subject of study and, in the case of the applied arts, ground this engagement in the experiential, or performative aspects of the creative workshops.

Before we go any further, try the following task. All you need is some time to reflect and a notebook or computer.

This task is to conduct a personal or self-ethnography. Don't worry if you don't know what that means yet. The steps are easy to follow and the explanation of ethnography will be heightened by your personal understanding. First, make a list of all your personal features – your gender, age, race, health, bodily characteristics, if you live alone, with a partner, married, if you are a parent or not, your self-image and something about your personality – are you shy, outgoing, etc. What is your personal history, how would you describe yourself? Explain your family history. Describe your career and its history. What are your expectations of your personal and professional development? What do you expect of others, how do they react to you? Describe your image of yourself. There may be other areas or questions that come to you, whatever comes, notice it, make notes (rather than judgements) for later reflections.

Next, spend some time reflecting on how the lists and stories you have compiled from the above task 'fit' with the culture in which you live and work (your neighbourhood, your workplace, region, country). Notice the differences between mass media images (television, magazines, etc.) of your gender compared to your own image of yourself. Notice the differences between your lists and stories and your perception of the general population in your sociocultural environment. Again, there may be other factors that are crucial for you to examine. The important aspect is that you give time and space to acknowledge whatever comes to. I am indebted to the work of Kealiinohomoku (1989) who outlines a 'praxis' for dance ethnology that begins with developing a self-ethnography. This task is developed from her work.

Once you have completed the task in the first text box you will have lists of data, the key to good ethnographic research. This data can be organised and collated to create stories, or ethnographic monographs (the term for the textual or visual representation of a group of people). Your aim is to try and develop as a reflexive researcher and this means being able to understand yourself within your psychological, sociological and cultural context. It is about being self-aware plus more than that. If, for example, you were to create an ethnographic monograph or performance from this data, or data from your fieldsite, it would mean that you are convinced that the data you have collated most completely represents the individual or group. The selection of material and subsequent interpretation are based on what seems to fit. This chapter begins to sketch out *how* it is we can *know* when the selection and its subsequent representation is right and appropriate. Some ethnographers would couch their findings in feminist, post-structuralist, phenomenological or other theoretical approaches. Others might be more inclined to say 'I have my theoretical approach which works with the data'. I am advocating that the researcher will know and have access to knowing when the findings are right and that knowing can be found in the body. Let's say it's a sensation of 'aha, yes, that's right, that's how it should be' that can be found in the body and can be developed. This process is more than a scientific measure against an external reality, it is an embodied knowing based on the experiential.

Damasio (1994) says that our bodies are used by the brain as a reference point for understanding our experiences of the world. He suggests that neural processes we experience as 'the mind' use the entire physical organism (tissues, membranes, organs – in other words the body and the brains) as a measure for understanding the world around us. Feelings, he says, may be located specifically in the body and become qualifiers for our experiences. So, for example, something happens that I perceive to be outside my body – like a smell or seeing someone who looks vaguely familiar – then I have a feeling in my body about that smell or that person, *and* I have a corresponding thinking part. In this way the feelings, which occur in the physical organism known as my body, are the sensors which indicate a match or otherwise with the current experience. Damasio (2000, p 41) says there is evidence to suggest that emotions play a key part in reasoning and decision-making. Because I experience the feeling and the thinking, although these are not usually separable aspects of the process and should not be understood by the reader as bifurcations in the Descartian sense, I am then able to say, 'yes that smells nice' or 'you look like someone I have met before'.

Knowing how we experience the world might allow us, as researchers, to understand our reactions and perceptions of each research environment better. This would mean being more reflexive. New opportunities in research may appear when we accept that emotions are not separable from the reasoning and decision-making processes. This can also be seen as a shift from a positivist to a post-positivist approach where the researcher, rather than discovering facts and measurable data, 'self-consciously selects data from a vast arena in order to determine what seems to be important or significant' (Green and Stinson, 1999, p 94) within a particular research context.

My bodily actions serve as the landscape through which I am able to think. My body has begun to experience the world differently because I have been engaged in the fieldsite, in circumstances that were previously unknown to me and now I have begun to experience my own world differently and so my landscape has shifted. It is the embodied reflexive practices in the fieldsite that have generated a need to *think* my world differently. Performance ethnography requires the researchers to take action in order to facilitate their own understanding. I can watch someone doing Oriental or Egyptian dancing and think I understand it. Only when I have attended and participated in an Egyptian dance class, felt the weight of the hip belt as it assists in the sway of my hips, will I have the embodied performative knowledge with which I can speak to and engage with the Egyptian dancers themselves. In this sense it is the action, the performative engagement that generates this new understanding.

Ok, now maybe you can take a moment to reflect on what you have just read. Put the book to one side and take a few deep breaths. Have you been reading for a long time? Have you given yourself time to take in, digest, all you have read today? Focus on the outward breath and begin to notice how you are sitting in your chair, if there is any tension held in your body. Let your attention move to whatever parts of your body seem to be drawing you and breathe into that body part. Try to let the tension go. Sometimes tightening the muscles first and then releasing them helps you to do this. Now, pick up the book again, and begin to read. This time you might try to notice how your body is reacting to the words on the page or what words and phrases seem to be drawing your attention. Allow this process to take its own journey and begin to notice how these words resonate within you. Is there a feeling of comfort or discomfort, puzzlement or engagement? Do you agree with me? Does this all seem like a silly idea? Can you locate your self-ethnography

---

within this writing in some way? Whatever your reaction, notice it and accept it, remembering you can and may choose to return to these thoughts and feelings at a later time. These ideas are developed from Gendlin's 'felt sense' (2003). For more information on this process you might usefully begin with the Internet (www.focusinginstitute.org). I will explain this approach in more detail as we progress.

These embodied experiences may not be easily translated into written form. Kirsten Hastrup, an anthropologist, says that researchers must work toward 'anthropological imagination'. This, she explains, is a process where the researcher should work toward a shift 'beyond the concept of the anthropological 'other' to the notion of 'anthropological imagination' (Hastrup, 1995, p 61). She goes on to suggest that to 'other' ourselves would 'necessitate the author speaking from a declared periphery, rather than centre, to create a world that is our fieldsite through the theorising that concentrates on making the world afresh, rather than getting it right' (Hastrup, 1995, p 10). There is not space here to discuss the problematic arena of 'othering' but to highlight the sociological, psychological and cultural complexities embedded in the dialectics of researcher and researched. In the process of considering her position in relation to her fieldsite, in this reconceptualised space, the anthropologist can begin to embrace the concept of 'ethnographic imagination'.

> I mean to emphasise the ethnographic as conditioning, grounding and setting the range of imaginative meanings within social thought. Ethnography provides the empirical and conceptual discipline. Ethnography is the eye of the needle through which the threads of the imagination must pass. Imagination is thereby forced to try to see the world in a grain of sand, the human social genome in a single cell. (Willis, 2000, pviii)

By embracing imagination, according to anthropologists and ethnographers, the researcher can begin to celebrate the task of writing as an imaginative act where the imaginative powers of the author give rise to the ethnography (Bacon, 2003, p 54). By embracing the notion of embodied reflexive practice the researcher can begin to explore their creative, imaginative and embodied interaction with the subject of study.

What is 'ethnography' and what is 'performance'?

Ethnography originated from anthropologists who used many variations of methodological approaches that were developed by researchers in other fields such as sociology, education, dance and performance. Common tools include participant observation, interviews, videoing and other research into the context of the selected field of study. There will be quantitative data such as how many participants, their age, gender, race, etc. but the qualitative data is usually considered to be the most useful for interpretation (Green and Stinson, 1999, p100). The conditions for discovery in a fieldsite vary. Techniques required may also vary from survey materials to use of the internet to intense participant observation. Primarily, ethnography is steeped in a belief in the research method of participant observation as a key tool that will be used to document an in-depth study of a group of people through the textual or visual image. What we are talking about here is doing what the participants are doing. This forms the basis for embodied knowledge in that participant observation assumes that data gathering will have a credibility if it is steeped in the experiences of our subject and, as researchers, we will be better equipped to understand and represent these experiences if we have participated and if we base our research in these experiences.

Whilst an expanding field of relations may appear endless, only a few of these relations in our fieldsite are 'activated and imbued with meaning by particular people' (Olwig and Hastrup, 1997, p9). If 'being in the field' (Rabinow, 1977, p 11) is not a pre-determined concept but one that involves attention to all potential moments, *regardless* of any pre-determined knowledge about the arts events, then the process of constructing the field needs explanation. Many applied arts researchers may be working in arenas where they believe the fieldsite is already constructed for them: a classroom for example. Amit suggests that the field site is a 'social category singled out by the author, rather than a self-conscious social group, who might be interacting with one another on an ongoing basis, independent of my intervention' (2000, p 14).

How are you doing? Let's try another 'focusing' task. Maybe you have been on the internet and found some information on 'focusing'. If not, do that now and, in particular, look for the introduction to the six steps of focusing. Having read through the steps, take yourself through a relaxation process such as I outlined in the previous task box. Begin to notice everything around you, outside of you (sounds, smells, the temperature, etc.). Then, slowly, begin to move your attention to the surface of your skin. How are you experiencing all those external sounds, smells, temperatures, etc? Then move further inward, to the inside of your body. Now gently begin to move through the six steps of focusing – clearing a space, felt sense, finding a handle, resonating, asking and receiving (Gendlin, 1981, pp 51-64). Remember you are not looking for answers or to analyse, you are developing an awareness of the felt sense, or the feeling in your body of a particular experience. Once you develop this skill you will be able to draw on it whilst you are conducting your fieldwork.

Performance is defined here as referring to a 'tangible, bounded event that involves the presentation of rehearsed artistic action' (Bial, 2003, p 57). Whilst drama education or other applied arts settings may only loosely fit into this definition, it is important to tease out the use of this term versus an alternative word that is much in favour currently in fields such as performance studies (see Schechner) (2002a, 2002b). This term is *performativity.* Bial indicates that performativity is similar in form and effect to a theatrical performance. Yet there are significant differences. He suggests that the term can be used by those not wishing to invoke the connotations of 'artificiality or superficiality that accompany the world 'theatrical'. 'Performative' can also refer to a specific philosophical concept concerning the nature and potential of language' (Bial, 2004, p 145). Bial's collection of essays on performance and performativity are useful places to deepen an understanding of the complexity of these terms. Performance and performative are problematic terms when placed in the frame of performance ethnography, although it is important to signal something of the creative aim of the methodology in its label. It would be appropriate to use either *performance*, because it implies that what is being researched is the presentation of rehearsed artistic action, or *performativity,* because it implies an agentic action in its broadest sense.

Before you begin the next section, take some time to reflect on what you have gleaned from the reading so far. Does it make sense yet? If not, how are you experiencing that in your body? Remembering it could be my writing just as much as it could be your ability to understand. Perhaps you are still just reading and not trying out these suggestions. That is ok too. I'm wondering how reading your way and trying out my suggestions might make your experience of the chapter different.

Research activity

This section describes the tasks undertaken by the conference delegates in order to show how this methodology might work in practice. As in the previous section there are examples that mirror or enhance those undertaken by the researchers. The account is written in the present to take you into the moment, to mirror the process itself.

At the initial meeting with the researchers I have assumed that they would come armed with knowledge about an ethnographic approach, most probably a positivist or scientific approach, and that my task would be to shift them to a more post-positivist approach (Green and Stinson, 1999) through my emphasis on interpretation and creativity. What quickly becomes evident is that these researchers are typical of many working in educational or applied arts settings: although they use tools similar to those found in an ethnographic methodology they do not consider themselves to be ethnographers. Many of the researchers tell me that 'research' in the applied arts needs a scientific edge in this age of accountability and that the application of a softer, more artistic approach might invalidate their research. This is a concern for anyone working with qualitative research methods. Ethnographers are always questing for appropriate representations of the fieldsite. They are also clear that whatever representation they create is steeped in the evidence they have discovered and is, as post-modernists would have it, mediated, fragmented, contestable and fluid. In other words, there is not one right answer but many perspectives and voices that represent various aspects of the fieldsite as it is experienced by the researcher at that moment in time. The chosen representation is relational in that the evidence or data is the result of what has been experienced between the researcher and her subject of study. Working with an ethnographic process requires the author to be creative within the constraints of the data collated.

Within a creative research environment such as the applied arts the researcher is compelled to work creatively in order to capture the essence of that fieldsite. Without this approach the creative environment will be omitted or discredited. If we tried to reformulate the case study in merely scientific and factual terms we would not be engaging in an ethnographic process that contains appropriate tools for the subject. The notion of appropriateness can and should be determined through an exchange with that fieldsite, rather than the researcher imposing a particular set of tools which may limit and determine the kind of research that can be gathered in that environment.

In my initial meeting with the researchers my primary concern was to make this creative aspect of the ethnographic process clear by setting tasks that would help them to develop this creative engagement through the bodily felt sense of situations. The felt sense, according to Gendlin is 'not vision, hearing, or touch, nor is it just the togetherness of the five senses. It is rather a direct bodily sense that you have and use all the time' (2003, p 103). It is more than a perception of something. It is a deep internal knowing that I ask the researchers to use as a research method within a highly physical research environment. The research station participants are all drama teachers, practitioners and researchers who rely on the felt sense to generate creativity in their work and so are able to comprehend the basic premise of this work. This process is like setting an improvisational task with a theme or idea as the stimulus and then asking the students how they 'felt' about the work they created.

To emphasise the role of the creative approach I continually ask the researchers to try and give their responses by talking through and with the body. One researcher said he had a 'squiffy' feeling inside and felt 'dislocated'. He could locate a meaning for this feeling and said this bodily sense let him know that he 'needs some context for this work, to know where we are going'.

We were going into a creative process that mirrors and elucidates the workshop practice the researchers watched each morning. During the observations, we sat in a circle, in a circular room, around the drama teacher and his participants and we studied the teacher's ap-

146

proach, we noticed body language, teaching techniques, the students' responses, and we also saw the other conference delegates who were visible in our distant vision.

You can do this task in any environment even if it isn't your chosen fieldsite. If you can participate in your fieldsite during this exercise you might think about how to adjust the task to suit that participation.

Whilst watching and experiencing your chosen subject allow yourself to watch whatever appears to draw your attention. You might like to make notes about what you see and how you are experiencing these activities. Don't worry about how you write notes at this stage, there will be time later on to examine and analyse your findings. Periodically you might like to draw your attention inside, to your body, to notice how you are feeling or what you are experiencing in your body. In this way you can begin to let the work emerge before you in a way that suits you by drawing on the ability to work with the felt sense of your experience. Again, you might like to note something of these experiences in your notebook and, again, don't worry about what you are experiencing as there will be time later to analyse these findings too.

During the research station sessions several researchers comment on the 'concentric circles of meaning' that were emerging in the workshop environment. These circles of meaning reflected the circular space where the workshops took place as well as the more metaphorical circles created by the constructed circumstance under scrutiny. These were not real eleven year olds in a real classroom. They were postgraduate students participating in a workshop designed for eleven year olds and they and the brave workshop leader Jonothan Neelands were watched, and encircled by over 100 conference delegates. Unlike a research project in a school or community setting we were not really looking at the work to understand how drama could empower young people, or how the gender relationships were altered because of the application of specific dramatic techniques to a real life situation. This was a constructed situation created to question and explore the possibilities of the research methodologies. This made the tasks doubly difficult as each task we set had many layers of meaning.

The researchers begin their research by allowing themselves to be drawn wherever rather than predetermine a particular theme or issue that might need elucidation. They looked at gender issues, noticed the power relationships in the proxemics, studied the hierarchical relationship between teacher and pupil and questioned the topics selected by the workshop leader for issues of race and gender stereotyping. Yet this was not our aim. We were not engaging in this task to analyse the workshop but to analyse the methodology. As we begin to explore our creative engagement and the felt sense of the workshop environment we notice how we resonate with certain aspects of the fieldsite. These are some of the comments from this early stage in the research: 'A good pedagogy, he knows a plan that is exciting', 'This is an inquiry, a shared journey', 'The teacher is looking to find out 'where can I take them', 'There are levels in operation', 'The leader is using his voice to put the group at ease', 'Like a bee and a honey pot (the workshop leader) is buzzing around the space seeing where the work is being made'. These comments are useful and highlight the group's primary focus on pedagogy but also reveal an objective view of the creative process. I ask them to find a way to express something of what they were drawn to in a way that did not rely on words. I suggested they might like to draw, or write poetically, or perform a response to the work they had seen. I continually ask the researchers to try and suspend their impressions and interpretations of the workshop and to replace a process of analysis or evaluation with one of creative enquiry in order to see what new information or experiential knowledge might emerge.

From your experiences of your fieldwork in the previous task try and find creative modes of expression. These should reflect what you experienced. Try not to worry too much in the first instance about what the participants might need in that representation. Your first task is to be clear about how you experienced it. Like the research station participants you might like to try drawing, poetry or perhaps the fieldsite had its own creative tasks and exercises. If so, try altering and adapting them. Notice how you feel as you undergo this process. What is the 'felt sense' of this discovery, of the creative process? Be sure to note down these responses to the task in whatever way seems to feel right (again, this might be another layer of creativity, like a creative response to the response).

This task generates drawings and short poems. The researchers notice that these drawings reflected the physical space such as floor patterns that highlight the proxemics, or more abstract images that reflect something of the social spatial relationships in the workshop. The researchers explain that they had not predetermined what they would draw and were surprised that an image created on the page, that emanated from a feeling they had whilst watching the workshop, appeared to convey accurately some deeper significance in a way they had not thought about. One woman drew a beautiful large eye and wrote these words 'Down through time I watch you; I speak to you and see you learn your own truths'. This symbolised, she later told us, something of the layers of viewing or the concentric circles of meaning, as well as the idea of the researcher needing to be the all-seeing eye, the one who can 'know' everything. She explained that she hadn't really been aware that she felt so strongly about her responsibility as researcher and that this task had helped her to clarify a personal position.

As the researchers explore the bodily felt sense of their experience of viewing the workshops they try out creative responses to the work they have seen and reflect on these responses, using their embodied reflex practice. We work toward understanding how our personal values and assumptions operate in relation to the fieldsite. Working from the felt sense, or through experience, is intended to heighten the researchers understanding of their role within the construction of knowledge.

As each day proceeds the researchers begin to notice and try out the dramatic techniques employed in the workshops. There is the use of canon, repetition, shadowing, and body sculpture employed metaphorically to assist the researchers in their understanding of a given text or image. In addition to these dramatic techniques they also highlight the following themes in the workshop;

- the nature of the student teacher relationship

- the gender- and social-typing which may exist within the group both in teacher student and student-student interactions

- the use of symbols/metaphor/shapes to make meaning as set by the teacher and as discovered in our notetaking processes

■ the relationship between all these aspects and the overall aesthetic of the work created.

What was not clear at this stage was how all these aspects were linked.

> The next task is to return to your data. That is the material you have generated through participant observation or observation in your fieldsite as well as your data from your self-ethnography. At this stage you should analyse what you have documented by looking for themes or general concepts that need further elucidation. When you have a list, such as the one compiled by the researchers, return to the field to deepen your understanding of these particular areas. You might need to include other tools such as interviewing, informal discussions as well as more creative tasks such as the ones you have already undertaken.

For the next two days the researchers work in small groups using these four headings to focus their research. They take a similar approach as before, noticing both the experience occurring outside the body in the workshop and their own bodily feeling of this experience. Then, using the felt sense of that experience as a starting point, to find a way to note, draw or perform something from that experience. The group begins to employ many of the dramatic techniques used in the workshops. From this exploration they start to believe that they are refining their four themes into two and that these two aspects to the workshop should form the basis of their representation.

The first theme is that the techniques being used in the workshops are being applied to assist the participants' discussion about a particular social or cultural topic in relation to their own world experiences. The participants are being asked to experience a situation in order to clarify or alter their ideological position. The researchers note that this is similar to their own research process: they too have been discovering the felt sense of an experience through their application of creative techniques. The second theme is the flow and dynamic use of space in relation to a notion of insider/outsider. It is noted that 'the aesthetic is only operating when the medium is exposed and running, in other words only when it is a piece (of theatre)' but that the 'way of doing something' was clearly located with 'direct and indirect leadership, tableaux, ideal of artistic integrity' and these were linked to an 'aesthetics of teaching – pace, flow, dynamics'. The researchers argue that the 'art form is based in the language separate from everyday aesthetic'. Many of the observed tasks set for the participants were based on the students' personal experiences but we were still 'stepping into a fictional world' that some of the researchers believed had a 'social conformity and an unspoken accepted language where questions about who gets heard and who doesn't were implicit and non-negotiable'.

In the combination of these two themes the group discover that the socio-cultural and gender politics in the workshop environment are heightened by the use of particular topics for study and that these gender and socio-cultural issues were evident in the application of particular creative or dramatic techniques and also in the subsequent creation of performance work created by the participants. It is beyond the scope of this chapter to give the full findings and analysis from the research environment. What is crucial is that by using the creative techniques seen in the workshop and enhancing and developing them, the researchers find connections between the creative practice and larger theoretical concerns within the fieldsite.

The final stage in this research process is the representation of the findings. Unlike the creation of a representation from the findings from a fieldsite, this particular instance requires the group to feedback on the effectiveness of their chosen methodological approach, rather than on particular findings from the workshop. Based on this, the group decides it would be impossible to give feedback in any other way than the process of doing that had been their staple diet throughout the week. In a day-long session the group works in what could only be recognised as a devising process, to create a performance from the creative techniques they had developed. What is generated in that performance is a creative response to a creative process where recognisable dramatic techniques provide the form whilst the research process provides the content. The process of drama education is reliant on dramatic techniques that allow the participants to see their world differently, or to make meaning for their lives. This is what appears to be happening in this workshop and it is also happening within the research station. The drawings, poetry and performed tasks allow us to move the image of concentric circles and the all seeing eye into an analysis of both the workshop and the ethnographic process. In this way the research begins and concludes with the creative, performative aspects for all concerned and generates new possibilities for the language of representation.

Other possibilities for performance ethnography

How are you doing? It's now six months later and I'm sitting at my computer, reflecting on the work undertaken during that intense week. There is a hesitation, some uncertainly, as I reflect upon the process. What did the research station participants learn? What did I learn? What do I think of the methodology? These questions buzz around in my head as I struggle to find a place where I feel at ease with this writing. I am looking for that 'aha' moment when I know I have the right words to describe what I mean. Umm… and you? What do you think so far? Where are you coming from? Do your experiences of performance, the arts or ethnography sit easily with this approach, are you resistant, or is there something else? Can you check with the bodily felt sense? How does it feel when I ask you these questions?

My dance and ethnography background means that I am always looking at the participants in order to understand what they do and why they do it, but also at the 'it' they are doing in order to find ways to articulate the experience of that thing being done. This means trying to find strategies to articulate the aesthetic concerns of particular artistic practices. I suspect this happens in other art forms. It happens in the world of dance because dancing is so often not articulating something that can be related to our everyday experiences and so the meaning – making strategies we might want to employ don't work when we try and ask 'what does that dance mean' when what was offered was abstract line and form presented by a human figure. People attempt to make sense of the world around us by relating our outer experiences of the world to our particular frame of references or personal set of experiences. This might mean that we relate artistic events to our everyday lives in our search for meaning. We can alter the way in which we can understand something through a similar artistic or creative engagement. This is the basic premise of participant observation: we will know something differently through our active engagement with that something. Yet most ethnographers still revert to the use of language, the written word, to represent what we have discovered. I am not suggesting we don't use language to do this. I am suggesting there is another step in the process.

The research station participants engaged in a three stage process. Stage one was the development of a reflexive approach through the heightened awareness of the felt sense in order to clarify the researchers' role within the process of research. The second was the actual fieldwork, or the collation of data from the fieldsite. The third was the representation of that data to the other conference delegates. This final step may have disrupted the natural flow of the research process in order to find suitable modes of representation for that context, rather than allowing the process, which would include the participants in the field, to determine the appropriate mode of representation.

In other contexts the process might take on a different guise. In the second phase the researcher should attempt to find out why particular characteristics of a form or genre are important to a group of people, how they structure and express this form/genre and how the group wish to be represented. This can be achieved in a variety of ways: video, drawing, poetry, words, etc. The relationship between the activity and the mode of representation must be considered in order for the researcher to select what they believe to be the best tool for the job. It may be that experimentation is necessary. Trying out similar techniques or ideas that are apparent in the fieldsite such as painting, improvisation, the use of metaphor, or forum theatre will allow the researcher to know the work afresh and differently. Only when these possibilities have been explored performatively can the researcher more fully understand the implications of their choice of representation.

 The third phase will then be determined by the second. Material and data collated in the previous phase will need to be analysed, looking for themes, congruencies and the like. In this phase I would recommend returning to the creative techniques or strategies found in the fieldsite in order to experience them again and again in your body, to know them through your bodily experiences. In this process they will begin to speak to you and through you rather than you allowing them to be othered. When you know them like you know yourself, you can begin to find suitable representations and contexts for the presentation of your findings.

The final task is to use all the previous tasks to find the right representation for your data. This can be seen to be something of a creative response to your fieldwork data gathering. Study the material you have, respond creatively to it. Use the images you have or some of the material you have gathered as a starting point for a 'focusing' task. Do this by doing or looking at the material until something inside you calls your attention. Allow your attention to rest on that bodily response. Acknowledge this feeling in your body. You might like to draw a picture, dance, act, etc. your felt response. I would suggest that applying similar theatrical, creative and aesthetic tasks to this stage of the process will ensure you remain true to the needs of your participants rather than moving into your creative frames of reference.

Repeat this process for as long as it takes to feel that the choices about a representational style and theme are right for your material. You may also like to try this process with the participants. They do not need to know about focusing to do this. You can ask them if what you are intending to do or say feels right to them. Of course, there may be ethical issues here so be sure you have worked through this aspect prior to this task.

Conclusion

Within the field of drama education there is a commitment to the idea that understanding comes from *doing* the thing itself rather than only reflecting on a thing done. This is similar to ethnographers who focus on dance and performance, who believe that the dance or performance event can be best understood through the use of participant observation, wherein the researcher uses her own knowledge of the discipline to assist her in the research (see Kaeppler, Williams, Farnell, 1994, Varela, 1995). Whenever I join a group to do fieldwork, that group others me as much as I have othered them. Each encounter is constructed in notions of self-ness and other-ness. This process allows populations under study to appear exotic and unfamiliar. This, according to Hastrup, has created a paradox where the subject of study and the researcher must appear equal, without objectification, in order to remedy the imbalance of the colonising subject, anthropology, towards a more balanced and harmonious global view of the anthropological world (1995, p 7). The result creates a difficulty for ethnographers, who must, by the nature of the task, write or document their findings and in this process, transform and objectify the subject. Perhaps this distance between self and other might better be understood as part of the process of self-representation (Pink, 2000, p 102). The link to performance ethnography is that the value of the research is to be found in the doing and this acts as a means towards reflecting upon the thing done. Another similarity is a belief that the subject of study may have more to say to us than our current frames of reference can allow us to access. We are looking to be able to articulate the feeling of the experience of both researcher and researched. We may be missing the point if we rely on our previous perception of the world and don't find tools and strategies for moving into the world of the participants in order to see things differently.

> That's it. I'm finished now. Maybe you would like to put the book down. Close your eyes and take a few deep breaths. Maybe you could make time to go for a walk or do some other pleasurable task whilst you reflect on the words in this chapter. How do you feel about what I have suggested? Can you acknowledge and feel that your body is the landscape for your reasoning? Has a creative approach to your ethnographic process altered what you have come to know? I'd like to know.

Recommended Reading

Damasio, A(2000) *The Feeling of What Happens: Body, Emotion and the making of Consciousness*, Vintage, London

Gendlin, E. (1981) *Focusing*, 2nd Edition, Bantam, New York

(*the original focusing guide that explains how to use the deepest level of awareness within your body*)

Hammersley, M. and P. Atkinson (1973) *Ethnography: Principles and Practice*, London, Routledge

(*a good and unproblematic introduction to ethnography*)

Hastup, K. (1995) *A Passage to Anthropology*, London, Routledge

Keeliinohomoku, J.W. (1989) 'Variables that affect Gender Actions and Reactions in Cootz, Y. (ed..), Dance Ethnology Fieldwork: A Praxis' in *UCLA Journal of Dance Ethnology*, Vol. 13, pp 48-53

(*this article has informed the development of tasks to develop a reflexive approach*)

Pocock, D. (1994) 'The Idea of a Personal Anthropology' in *Journal for Anthropological Study of Human Movement*, vol. 8(1), pp 11-28

(*another key text in thinking about how to locate yourself within your research*)

Schechner, R. (2002b)'Fundamentals of Performance Studies' in Stucky, N. and C. Wimmer (eds.) *Teaching Performance Studies*, USA: Southern Illinois Press, pp ix-xii

> (*Schechner problematises the notion of performance and well as discussing notions of the performative*)

References

Amit, V. (ed, 2000) *Constructing the Field: Ethnographic Fieldwork in the Contemporary World*, London, Routledge

Bacon, J. (2003) 'Unveiling the Dance: Arabic Dancing in an Urban English Landscape', unpublished PhD, University of Surrey

Bacon, J. (2005) 'The role of ethnography in the practice of Performance Studies in the UK' in *The Practice of Performance Studies in the UK, Issues in Theatre and Performance*, Intellect

Bial, H. (2004) *The Performance Studies Reader*, New York, Routledge

Browning, B.(1995) *Samba: Resistance in Motion*, Bloomington, Indiana University Press

> (*a good example of an ethnography that tries to represent the felt sense of the dancing*)

Buckland, T. (1999) *Dance in the Field: Theory, Methods and Issues in Dance Ethnography*, London, Macmillan

> (*a good text for examining methodological issues*)

Cornell, A. W. (1996) *The Power of Focusing: A Practical Guide to Emotional Self-Healing*, New York, MJF Books

> (*an introduction to Focusing*)

Damasio, A. (1994) *Descartes' Error: Emotion, Reason, and the Human Brain*, New York, Harper Collins

> (*an expert on neurophysiology of emotions*)

Damasio, A. (2000) *The Feeling of What Happens: Body, Emotion and the making of Consciousness*, London, Vintage

Farnell, B. (1994) 'Ethno-Graphics and the Moving Body', in *MAN*, Vol. 29(4), pp 929-974

Farnell, B. (1995) 'Introduction' in Farnell, B. (ed.) *Human Action Signs in Cultural Context: The Visible and Invisible in Movement and Dance*, London, Scarecrow Press, pp 1-28

Farnell, B. (2000) 'Where Mind is a Verb: Spatial Orientation and Deixis in Plains Indian Sign Talk and Assininboine (Nakota) Culture' in Williams, D. (ed.) *Anthropology and Human Movement: Searching for Origins*, London, Scarecrow Press, pp 77-93

> (*Farnell is a key researcher who works to develop modes of representation where the dancing can 'speak'*)

Fox, R. (ed, 1991) *Re-capturing Anthropology: Working in the Present*, New Mexico, School of American Research Press

> (*this is an interesting text as it highlights many issues in contemporary anthropology such as the problematic nature of creating representations based on partial truths*)

Garner, S. B. Jnr. (1994) *Bodies Spaces: Phenomenology and Performance in Contemporary Drama*, Cornell University Press

> (*this text is quite old now but gives an idea of the use of phenomenology in contemporary drama, it is a useful starting point for understanding experience in creative environments*)

Gendlin, E. (2003) 'Beyond Postmodernism: from concepts through experiencing' in Frie, R. (ed), *Understanding Experience: Psychotherapy and Postmodernism*, London, Routledge, pp 100-115

> (*this is an interesting collection of essays on experience but the reader needs to be prepared for the focus on psychotherapy*)

Green, J. and S. W. Stinson (1999) 'Postpositivist Research in Dance' in Fraleigh, S. H. and P. Hanstein, *Researching Dance: Evolving Modes of Inquiry*, London, Dance Books, pp 91-123

> (*this edited text has other interesting approaches to research*)

Keeliinohomoku, J.W. (1989) 'Variables that affect Gender Actions and Reactions in Cootz, Y. (ed..), Dance Ethnology Fieldwork: A Praxis' in *UCLA Journal of Dance Ethnology*, Vol. 13, pp 48-53

> (*this article has informed the development of tasks to develop a reflexive approach*)

Okely, J. (1992) 'Anthropology and Autobiography: Participatory experience and embodied knowledge' in Okely, J. and H. Callaway (eds.), *Anthropology and Autobiography*, London, Routledge, pp 1-28

Olwig, K.F. and Hastrup, K, *Sitting Culture: The Shifting Anthropological Object*, London, Routledge, 1997

Pink, S. 'Informants' who come 'home'' in Amit, V. (ed.), *Constructing the Field: Ethnographic Fieldwork in the Contemporary World*, London, Routledge, 2000, pp 96-119

Probyn, E (1993) *Sexing the Self: Gendered Positions in Cultural Studies*, London, Routledge, 1993

Rabinow, P. (1977) *Reflections on Fieldwork in Morocco*, Berkeley: University of California Press

Schechner, R. (1977)*Performance Theory*, London, Routledge

Schechner, R. (2002a) *Performance Studies: An Introduction*, London, Routledge

Stanley, L. and S. Wise (1990) 'Method, methodology and epistemology in feminist research processes' in Stanley, L. (ed), *Feminist Praxis*, London, Routledge, pp 20-62

Varela, C. (1995) 'Cartesianism Revisited: The Ghost in the Moving Machine or in the Lived Body. An Ethnogenic Critique' in Farnell, B. (ed) *Human Action Signs in Cultural Context: The Visible and Invisible in Movement and Dance*, London, Scarecrow, pp 216-293

Willis, P. (2000) *Ethnographic Imagination*, London, Polity

> (*a social scientist embraces aspects of artistic into the ethnographic process*)

Woolcot, H. (1995) *The Art of Fieldwork*, London, Alta Mira

Yordon, Judy E. (1997) *Experimental Theatre: Creating and Staging*, Prospect Heights, Illinois Waveland

8

Post-structuralist 'Methodology'

Ian McCormick

Structuralist theories appear to generate a systematic and stable approach to making meanings. It's not that difficult to work out paired oppositions. Yet you may find yourself dissatisfied: can we really reduce the complexity of making meaning to tops and bottoms, male and female, black and white? Post-structuralism promises less, but performs more. Rather than a system of meaning, a post-structuralist favours singularities of expression that undermine system by questioning its schematic temperament. Any short definition is prone to simplification, and the whole project is preoccupied by the elusiveness of tangible or fixed meanings. So acquaintance with post-structuralism may be frustrating: what is to be done with it? Post-structuralism both exceeds and falls short of any methodology that attempts to structure it. It's as slippery and elusive as art itself! Its starting point is an obsession with destabilising definitions and distinctions. The research station transactions out of which this chapter emerged were therefore close encounters with the prescribed keynote theme of the IDIERI 2003 conference: 'destabilising definitions and distinctions.' This chapter seeks to demonstrate that deconstruction is far less alien than it first appears.

Post-structuralism is a bewildering combination of theoretical projects and their applications. I argue that elements of the post-structuralist approach afford the possibility of an open and balanced approach to the twin dynamics of criticism and creativity; post-structuralism folds one into the other. Underpinning my methodology is the sense that both criticism and creativity are required in the shifting process of performance and are inseparable as the twin strands of participatory drama. Moreover, a post-structuralist approach serves to interrogate all conventional binaries such as teaching/learning, or acting/observing. More than just turning them upside down or reversing them, a post-structuralist would uncover the trace, play or spectre of the one inside the other. Accordingly, post-structuralism employs an exhilarating rigour to critical and creative work that involves individual and group, word and world. The primary obsession of post-structuralism is a disproportionate scrutiny of limits of (non)-meaning. Before attempting some practical exercises it is important to grasp the tangible and the elusive elements of the theory.

Post-structuralist methodology is not a reductive set of procedures to be committed to memory, translated, and applied to multiple contexts. Rather it attaches itself to the singularity of any dramatic moment: its educational component, in its moment of unfolding. Post-structuralism deploys an elusive alchemy in always moving beyond that moment as something that can be re-presented on demand. The alchemist was an early species of chemist whose experiments could be repeated with identical results each time they were attempted. For performance, as for post-structuralism, there is no step-by-step rulebook or chemical recipe for success. These statements are rather precautionary and frustrating, primarily because they leave so much open to critical performances as processes that cannot be translated into quantifiable measures of success or failure. Rather than aiming for closed outcomes in our experience of drama, post-structuralism approaches re-presentation as shifting, tactical and incomplete. The aim is a super-consciousness of how performance affects ideas, events, beliefs and intuitions.

Post-structuralist approaches correspond to Marvin Carlson's notion of performance that 'undoes the competencies, codes, and structures of the theatrical ... to allow a free flow of experience and desire' (1996, p137). Post-structuralism studies our constructedness as shifting subjects in terms of power inequalities such as gender and sexuality, colour, creed, age, disability. None the less, deconstruction typically opens up and moves beyond binary oppositions. As a response to structuralism, deconstruction has two stages: reversal and displacement. There is a reversal of a binary opposition, which is also a violent hierarchy such as master/slave or black and white, followed by a reorientation, or displacement of the problem, to avoid repetition. It is insufficient for the master and slave simply to swap roles. In a radical and challenging sense, the drama process signalled by 'as if' must face its other 'as if *not*' and find traces of meaning across and between the terms A post-structuralist would also ask to whom the performance is addressed, and question the omniscient narration, authentic voice, romantic identification and notions of realism. In terms of staging an event or a performance outcome, post-structuralism would tactically privilege synchronicity or chance over a logical cause-effect scenario. Such an approach demands that we elicit with rigour our most unacknowledged assumptions and our veiled points of vantage; vision and blindness are necessarily intertwined. The rest of the chapter describes how we went about *doing* deconstruction within post-structuralism and assesses its critical and creative value for performance practice.

Contexts and questions

The primary purpose of the research station was to facilitate daily critical reflection on the pedagogic practice and conceptual assumptions of the teaching practice observation that preceded it. In so far as a prior methodology was to be employed, and research tools provided, the critical label attached to the research station was post-structuralist approaches. Without knowing in advance the nature of the morning practice observations, I had sketched out a variety of interlinked post-structuralist themes and preoccupations for discussion:

- destabilising drama
- moving beyond binary oppositions
- queering sexuality
- deconstructing subjects and subjectivities
- customs, rules and power
- margins, hybrids and the centre

Notions of power, representation and performance were evident from the outset as intertwined issues that might be explored in terms of the conference's theme. To be more specific, several aspects of a deconstructive project, loosely derived from the work of Derrida, were also at work, and tactically deployed throughout the period of research: supplement/supplant; frames; *jouissance*/play; the trace; haunting/spectrality. Once grasped in some degree, these deconstructive approaches lend themselves to a variety of contexts. This chapter describes a selection of shorter activities undertaken in the research station and their relevance to the case study. As I was in role as deconstructive facilitator I do not claim to re-present the group experience in whole or even in part. I merely offer basic proposals for developmental activities to help explore post-structuralism in relation to performance. Where I risk speculation and definition you will soon begin to see that with a gentle theoretical nudge further deconstruction is possible!

Initial discussion in our research station was based on the question 'Drama is … ?' followed by 'Theory is … ?' The aims were to limber up, to gain a sense of the diversity of experience in the group, to uncover ways of thinking and imaginative directions at work within the research station. To the relief of many members our time was not spent head down in textual analysis of the recommended reading. It seemed clear early on, given a degree of confidence and risk-taking, that each individual would trace out her own theoretical direction. Playful and open-ended, ungrounded in ideological priorities, correctness or pseudo-scientific results, discussion of definitions was free-floating. A trifling detail might be subjected to serious analysis; comic arrows deflated issues of great importance. Theory was like a window: it framed what we saw. Consequently, the view opened by one window might be closed by another. So how do theories frame or contain? Are they just pictures of the world taken from pre-determined angles? In starting to deconstruct there is a vertigo effect: what is left to hold on to? On reflection, the variety and complexity of approaches was excessive, rather like multiple mental roller-coasters! Debates moved in too many directions and on too many levels. There were too many lines of flight, textures, seams, and gaps to the point of narcissistic irresponsibility. Sceptical elements in the research station wanted to know what was the value of post-structuralism, even, what were its ethical values? It seemed as though we were putting deconstruction on trial, or at least to the test.

Distrust and suspicion are not uncommon; deconstruction has earned itself many enemies through its dark and unintelligible pronouncements. For critical detractors such as John M. Ellis, deconstruction's ethical claims are exaggerated and sham: 'Accordingly, there is heavy emphasis on moral terminology in deconstructive writings. Deconstruction is 'disturbing,' 'disruptive,' it 'unmasks,' 'subverts,' 'dismantles,' 'exposes,' 'challenges,' and, a favourite word, it is a 'scandal'' (1989, p140). In relation to its usefulness, was deconstruction promising more than it could perform?

Another question recurring in early discussion was to ask why we failed to provide working definitions of the theory in a couple of jargon-free sentences. Also, what was the relevance to drama of deconstruction's approach to Plato, Kant, Nietzsche, Heidegger? We seemed to be locked into a deep philosophical debate about nothing! John M. Ellis provides a fitting summary: 'the sense of belonging to an intellectual elite, of having left behind the naivete of the crowd, of operating on a more sophisticated intellectual plane than that crowd.' (1989, p151) Yet what is the fate of anything, if its aesthetic destiny could be judged in a couple of sentences? If we defined *Hamlet* or *King Lear* thus, what would be missing, unheard, unwritten? In post-structuralism's insistence on deep mercurial veins of interpretation, critical freedom and rigour as the condition of language and being, don't we encounter the scandal, the truth of our true condition, that truth/ meaning will not stay present to us, it is always slipping away? Our situation might be that described by John M. Ellis's sceptical critique of deconstruction: 'It would be like looking at a box that has never been opened and never will be opened and saying that there is something valuable in it. Maybe – but how could we know?' (1989, p4) Our research station promised to destabilise definitions but deconstruction seemed to be offering a 'Nothing will come of nothing' solution that was, to say the least, unsatisfactory.

Broadly, aspects of the initial research station scenario were symptomatic of the post-modern performance condition; what Cecily O'Neill has called 'the fragmentation and distribution of roles among the group, non-linear and discontinuous approach to plot, the reworking of classic themes and texts, a blurring of the distinction between actors and audience.' (1995, pxvii) With regard to the broader contexts and our group's sense of the widening circles that rippled out and back to their origin, beyond the institutional framework, David Booth has noted that 'Drama is an ubiquitous force in our present world, an everyday and everywhere occurrence...' (2003, p18)

Throughout the week, contexts, break-ins and -outs would fracture the closed safety of the research station. We would put things in boxes, take them out, conceal and reveal. On a detour of meaning, the box, like the frame, or the circle, elopes between its inner and outer spaces.

I am conscious that the outline provided so far has already set alarm bells re-sounding. Certainly a chorus of disapproval, supplemented by silent scepticism and tentative engagement, were some of the initial interventions manifested in the first session, a prologue or pre-text to the stations that set for the following day, when the case-study and research station shifted up a gear. The prefatory readings proposed were judged to be labyrinthine critical nonsense and provided a focus for general discontent. In our open-ended discussion, however, we were not ... locked in a cage with Marvin Carlson's *Performance* (1996), Cover Photograph 'Two Undiscovered Amerindians Visit Madrid'; nor were we precariously balancing Mark Fortier *Theory/Theatre* (1997), Cover Photograph 'Scarabeus' Stilt Walkers' ...The inadequacy of theory texts in general, coupled with what appeared to many as the self-indulgent and frivolous private language games of post-structuralist performance theory helps to explain the grave doubts expressed by practitioners against these deconstructing wizards.

Yet those moments in drama when we see into the life of things and simultaneously our hold on values is momentarily placed in parenthesis excite a human desire for deep reflection that is just as demanding as any conceptual box of tricks offered by theory. I am not arguing for an equality in opposition of theory and practice but for a renewed sense of the one always already inside the other, such that the notion of priority has been abolished. It is mildly improper to demand complexity in art and simplicity in theory, for such an unbalanced binary opposition devalues the terms involved. Deconstruction helps to explore the spacing between the possibility and the impossibility of making meaning, or what might be called telling the truth.

My own experience was derived from teaching literary theory to first year undergraduates. I was familiar with the resistance to theory from common-sense, plain English opponents. Also a sense of strangeness: how could we entertain the foreign body of theory, given that the first impulse was an indignant rejection of the need to attend to it. I was also conscious that each of us was playing roles and indulging in power games partly beyond our control. Such is the nature of institutional power. Moreover, the process of disrupting the underlying binary of opposition/resistance and engagement/conversion was crucial to unlocking the alchemical potential of theory as performance.

Working with post-structuralism

Following a structuralist procedure we undertook an initial critical/creative exercise for 5-10 mins. One half of the group had to describe all the associations for them of 'Day' and the other 'Night' on flipcharts using keywords. Any keywords will do but it is important in the initial stage not to enter into terms that already have too obvious an ideological agenda such as master/slave. We had not yet observed Jonothan Neeland's teaching work and did not know one another well, so we were stumbling in the dark, awaiting enlightenment! The outcome was as follows:

DAY	NIGHT
Bright	Space of possibilities
Revealing	Letting go
Open	The dreaming
Public	The ending of today
Productive	Is half a mill wheel that can only
Beginning	turn one way
Awake	Is never ... the clock ticks 3 a.m.
Enabling	Is a written text like the marks of
Allows possibilities	a pen against the stars
Opportunities	Is finding light in the dark
Dealing with stuff	Is relaxing; friendly, frightening
Pressure	Is solitude
Exposed	Is quiet
Frightening	Dreaming visions
Removes possibilities	Rest and relaxation
Challenges	
Demands	

Binary oppositions occur everywhere; they seem to generate and position meanings, discourses, and ideologies. In the most arbitrary sense they let us know we are here, because we are not there. Or, we are here, because we are not (t)here. Meaning is simply a system of differences. More important, as a supplement to the structuralist approach, was the next stage of the exercise. This requested members of the group to identify the terms which appear on both sides, the descriptive features that lack a clear-cut opposition and those that appear to be displaced from their proper position. As one of the NIGHT group wrote, we were 'finding light in the dark.' Even opposites have an uncanny untruth considered as poetic paradoxes or oxymorons, such as, darkness visible, bitter sweet etc. At this stage word associations and analogical or metaphorical thinking were empowering members of the oppositional groups to operate across the binary divide, we had begun to experience the gap across which traces of meaning flow or solidify.

If such simple words as Day/Night are so slippery as a way of organising meaning, their opposition sometimes a sameness, what repercussions were there for other binaries, indeed all binaries? What happens when we 'erase' Day/Night and paste over Sun/Moon; Male/Female; Culture/Nature; Master/Slave; Rehearsal/ Spontaneity? Do the same metaphoric associations hold? Meaning is not eradicated, but its truth is somehow told by constantly shifting metaphors. Notice also the unstable chain of associations contained in Day-Sun-Male-Culture-Master and place these against the traces of meaning linked through Night-Moon-Female-Nature-Slave. It would be interesting to try these on A *Midsummer Night's Dream* or *The Tempest*. Our encounter with the free play of signifiers shifted us painlessly from the confines of structuralism to the free-play of post-structuralism. Note that the semantic relation is less one of signifier to signified (*word* night to *concept* night) than of signifier to signifier, thus implying a deferral or postponement of the meaning onto the next signifier in the chain. Meaning fails to reach a terminus, or an origin, that might serve to anchor its free play of associations. The meaning of the word Woman is not a *simple* opposition to the signifier chain Day-Sun-Male-Culture-Master. Neither is it uniquely identified with Night-Moon-Female-Nature-Slave, though many of these operated as metaphoric constructions in culture: they perform ideological functions that appear to ground order and meaning together as natural. They are less fixed the more we see their slippery metaphors. Basically deconstruction makes meaning more provisional; like performance in motion it serves to open meaning to critical and creative play.

It was proposed that theories are windows, or frames of vision. On the second day we reflected on these in terms of the practice observation, and the conference world as a performance scenario. The frame does not simply contain nor is it simply the inner situatedness of the event: it looks outward to the social and cultural institutions, to their discourses and textures. We were beginning to ask post-structuralist questions: is the frame part of the performance, is it in the picture? In which spaces is the performance unlimited? The teaching observed included all these: the participating students observed themselves, observed each other as individuals and groups, were observed by their teacher, as we observed them, a widening circle of teachers learning, observing the reactions of the observers, as individuals and groups, watched through the windows at times by other summer school students, who were momentarily watched by us. Looking back, moments recalled to life in the spectral group memory of the research station, in conversations over dinner, in the bar, by email, observed again on video, and so returning, with a difference, a deferral of the event, the moment, the trace, lost now in an endless chain of signifiers. Events, like texts, function as chains of significations. Where and how do we enter the picture, or even exit what happens?

The notion of meaning as trace or spectre, together with the case-study experience of the practice observation led us round and through discussion to *Hamlet*, especially the notion of a crisis that must be performed, the play-within-the-play, Hamlet's 'I am the observed of all observers.' Hamlet frames the ultimate binary 'to be, or not to be' then deconstructs its performed qualities and embarks on an impossible task for the living, the work of limitless mourning. As it turned out, the first workshop/performance case study by Jonothan Neelands (scene from *Antigone*) was concerned with Life/Death, Inside/Outside. The participants achieved impressive creative responses in relation to elements of the dramatic situation: the dead unburied body of Polynices, the city gates, Antigone and the crowd and the guard between worlds inside/outside the gates. The drama work of mourning was in itself a refusal of the simple binary oppositions: that the living must let go of the dead. The unreconciled poetic traces occur between the binary terms, and beyond them. Our focus for discussion, following through from the practice observation, was the importance of the guard at the Gates of Difference. The cultural containment of death as uncompleted funeral arrangements was a grotesque anomaly of war. The performers were asked: 'with all the time in the world, what would Antigone say to Kreon'? The power of the creative response springs in a sense from the time/timeless, truth/fiction, that we witnessed in performance. At times the prepared image that began the teaching session became a speaking, living picture. At others living performers froze to become a silent representation of a grotesque intuition. The shifting strategies employed did not require a post-structuralist critique, so much as already enact deconstructive tendencies.

The second day's case study was based around the story of a schoolboy called Pedro, and the participants'/actors' attempts to make sense of an essay he had written in a totalitarian setting called 'what we do at home'. The performance involved finding out what the letter told us about the child: his family, his teacher, his school, his society. The case-study was grounded in a building and revealing of contexts, not all of which were present at the outset of which he was part but which were to be re-presented in one form or another. Family freeze-frame scenarios were used as spectral enactments of ideological forces on human agents; again these were deconstructive traces, what Jonothan Neelands called 'caught-in-between moments'. The strategic fit between imaginative creativity and critical theory helped us to understand more profoundly the performed qualities of the teaching observation. The classroom observation, a classroom scenario, was a play-within-play. Other levels of performance and play were to be introduced in our research seminar as supplements. The authoritarian environment of the school was expressed in the statement that 'children would write more if there was silence'. From a deconstructive position we were alerted to the silence that inhabits all writing: the voice of dead authors, black marks on a page. And there were gaps in Pedro's diary-essay that sanctioned their sportive, playful interpretation in the performances.

As a supplement to these aspects of the teaching observation, our initial discussion tended to focus on the notion of rules, customs, laws and conventions, in the seminar space we occupied, in education, and beyond. We tried to voice the silent, unspoken, unwritten rules: the deconstructive lifeblood of the ideological monster. The research station's work involved considering supplementary rules designed to help discussion:

Community of enquiry rules for discussion:

- Let everyone have a turn at speaking
- Say nothing hurtful to someone
- Think before you speak
- One speaks – all listen: don't interrupt!
- People can 'pass' – say nothing if they wish
- Don't laugh unkindly at something someone has said
- Each group might like to add other rules

The research group was not altogether impressed: how could they really adopt or sanction someone else's rules? Surely rule seven offered the possibility of an opening for totalitarian overthrow? Given the carnivalesque energy and intellectual acumen at work in our research station, I thought we might design our own rules, one for each individual to submit anonymously to the group. No doubt there were efforts to identify authors, but part-ownership and part-anonymity make for excellent bedfellows in a performing scenario that deconstructs safety and risk. So here were the 'Golden rules':

Keep it structured – take turns if need be
Listen
Listen hard and don't talk too much
Only compromise if you believe it
Listen to everyone
Maintain a balance between honouring the flow of a discussion, and subverting/integrating it
No set-ups
Listen to the context of someone's question/comment
Don't block – keep open
That people are able to trust each other and value input
Enable others to formulate and express ideas that are new to them
Drawing on our own relevant understanding and experience to progress discussion
Be respectful of other members

The next stage (note the initial binary logic) was to design a set of anti-rules, known as the 'RED RULES'

Remember there is no right or wrong
Use sarcasm
Be smart
Be personal
You must take umbrage at least twice each session at something apparently inoffensive
Speak out loudly whenever you feel like it
If you disagree with someone, stop him or her from spouting off as soon as possible!
Be suspicious of everyone else's answer or comment
Ban all rules, set up your own
Be openly critical of others' ideas and work
Challenge ideas aggressively
Love me!

We placed the rules in two circles, anti-rules at the centre. The deconstructive game in this case first turns the opposition inside-out; then it identifies contradictions or similarities within each circle and between the circles. Ideological rules are not unwritten but unwritable; that is the power of an inescapable language system. Deconstruction admits that we cannot replace rules with anti-rules but it can empower a postponement of them by supplementing rules with more rules to the point of absurdity. The practice observation relating to Pedro's story had demonstrated related issues, several actors commenting on the writing concealed behind the rules and the ambiguous relation between the school and classroom's rules. A romantic or radical approach might seem to favour 'Red rules' but these can fold into something like a totalitarian cult of the individual compared to the more respectful agenda of consent of the 'Golden rules'. The deconstruction of inner/outer circles can be applied to other complex constructions such as sexuality. Thus: Outer: heterosexual, married, monogamous, procreative, non-commercial, in pairs, in a relationship, same generation, in private, no pornography, bodies only, and vanilla. Inner: homosexual, unmarried, promiscuous, non-procreative, commercial, alone or in groups, casual, cross-generational, in public, pornography, with manufactured objects, and sado-masochistic.

The more the circles widened – child, family, teacher, school, society – in Pedro's story and in the ongoing observation of Neeland's teaching, the more they narrowed through different ideological frames working back on the human/acting agent. Our mapping of these possibilities produced the following:

Subject/object
Subject of a sentence
British 'subject'
Subjection
Subject to the law
personality/character/identity
Ego-formation (Freud/Lacan)
Gendered, feminist, queer identities
Colonial (Foucault)
Economic; 'homo economicus'
Aesthetic (Joyce pictures, *see below*)

How can we trace subjects/ subjectivities, uncovering the traces of violence and power that have constituted them? How are they formed, constructed, acted out? We were entering branches of post-structuralism that deal with gender, psychoanalysis and postcolonial theory. Deconstructive critics are fascinated by the relations between the subject and its 'other' in traces, moments of time, tableaux and still life. Given that the drama we had experienced earlier in the day had made effective use of visual elements (source and supplementary material) and freeze frame enactments/modifications, my research station was asked to think through the multiple application of the above in relation to a swift succession of images, each with single subject, claiming to 're-present' James Joyce. Taken from Richard Ellman's biography (1984), the list of images may be summarised as:

Joyce's Death mask
Cesar Abin's portrait of Joyce as question mark (1932)
Desmond Harmsworth's 'Joyce at Midnight'
Joyce as singer
Brancusi 'Symbol of Joyce' (1929)
James Joyce in Zurich (1915) playing guitar, photo by Ottocara Weiss
Joyce's passport photograph, Paris.
Joyce in Zurich (1919)
'Asked what he was thinking about when C.P. Curran photographed him, Joyce replied, 'I was wondering would he lend me five shillings.'

The Joyces on their wedding day (with their solicitor) July 4, 1931, as they walk to the registry office in Kensington.
Drawing of Joyce by Wyndham Lewis (1921)

For a *dominant* specularity (way of seeing), representation aimed to fix Joyce's image, to establish his *identity* without doubt (death mask, passport); other ways of seeing were much more unstable (five shillings anecdote; Joyce as a curve, a symbol). In the violence of representation which was a core feature of Pedro's life and his society, the freeze frame struggled to depict versions that were 'same and also different' that balanced 'joining and parting' scenarios; Jonothan Neelands was asking for representations of the child's imaginary grotesque vision to be embodied; the monstrous expression of unspoken horror; the enactment of fear. At the end of the practice observation session, David Booth read the final sections of Pedro's story. Pedro had said in his essay that they played chess routinely at home in the evening. Apparently, this was coded reference to his parents as radicals against the totalitarian regime. They were engaged in tactical manoeuvres. They did not own a chess set, but would now have to buy one to validate their son's fictional story. The final lines of the story that 'complete' the deception make it true by adding a chessboard, for it is yet another move in an on-going game of power. There is always another game to win or lose; the human condition, like the deconstructive turn, is composed out of an infinite range of possible positions. Chess, like tragedy, is a noble and violent game that also employs comic deception (Hamlet).

The final section of the research station examined the relation between subject, stories, texts and history. As in the practice observation, the aim was to facilitate movement between self and society, world and word, by greater consciousness of the play of significations, especially those on the margins (e.g. queer or monstrous constructions.) Our aim was to gain a grasp of the 'new historicist' dislocation of a privileged subject at the centre of history and his replacement with a variety of voices, anecdotes and incomplete fragments, which are traces of 'History'. Part of the discussion also emerged from the 'Research Conversation' concerning Dorothy Heathcote's work and its spectral presence (transmitted through Gavin Bolton) under the title 'What is the truth in biography?' Initially, the exercise involved writing your most memorable ex-perience of a performance of *Hamlet*, the year and the place.

Having been folded and shuffled with random anonymity by members of the research station, these were placed in a long chain across the floor in chronological order. We then discussed them in order of the oldest memories first.

Versions of Hamlet: my most memorable experience of the play, with place and date:

'Yesterday. 'ghost ... cried like an oysterwife' from Arden edition of Hamlet'

'Recently. School. My classroom. Two students worked with poems in class. One presented orally 'To be'; another worked with visual art and represented the meaning of poem through: line, symbol, light, dark, shape, space. Surprised by the quality of the representation and the nature of it.'

'2003. University College Northampton. Ophelia's version of her story.'

'Almodi's Journey, dir. Runar Gundbrusson. 1997. Almodi is Icelandic for Hamlet. This performance was a physical journey, a promenade through a warehouse. I moved from one city to another, from one life to another: it opened an appreciation of 'other' types of performance – of visual images, which widened my world.'

'Canada. My Hamlets are overlapping traces, like ghosts on a television screen before cable. Keanu Reeves (1995) brought a strange but human presence to the youth of Hamlet. Richard Burton did a fine reading without character in a sense.'

'School Hall. March 1994. They are working in role – on the mousetrap scene. Children are jugglers, acrobats – and cooks preparing a banquet, which is cold meats. They tell me Claudius and Gertrude must like cold meats as they had it at their wedding. One girl is a serving maid. She offers food to Claudius, says, 'here you are Claudius, here is your cold meat'. She bows, moves to Gertrude 'here you are Queen Gertrude, here are your cold meats'. Hamlet is sitting next to them. The girl bows, solemnly and respectfully, 'here you are Prince Hamlet, eat up your chips'. A little later, I say to the girl – 'why did you give Prince Hamlet chips?' A little later she answered – 'poor Prince Hamlet, he needs a bit of cheering up.'

'Theatre Nymegen, 1983. My schoolmate being Hamlet (great actor at that time). Seeing and hearing his private life through his acting in a way that deepened the involvement. Big reviews that he was 'great' the journals wrote, but I only knew why. Hamlet did not act for years, he returned to the theatre in the last five years.'

'1982. My Hamlet is the story of Tyrone Guthrie directing a production in Minneapolis and learning early in the rehearsal that Ophelia was pregnant. His response was 'great, we'll use it.''

'The Other Place – Stratford, 1975. Buzz Goodbody/Ben Kingsley, $4^1/4$ hrs uncut. No interval. 'I am dead, Horatio' – poison gradually paralysing his body so he just started to feel his arm become paralysed (Goodbody's death/suicide) followed by Fortinbras violently pushing the outer and inner doors of the theatre open and a cold draught of air swept into the auditorium – sense of chill. Impact of the 'natural' in theatre.'

'My Hamlet is many Hamlets seen and possible Hamlets ... c. 1972 (31 years old). McKellen's chilling self-aware, gallows humour – posturing to the watchers.'

'c. 1965. Joseph Papp. Shakespeare in the Park. Central Park NY. Waiting in line, early afternoon. Beautiful day – sandwiches – blanket. Diversity of people. Modern dress – first for me.'

'c. 1962. Summer. Stratford. Christopher Plummer. Curtain call. He let us see his exhaustion (or playing at his exhaustion?). I remember the call. I have wiped (or rather it has wiped) the (his) performance from my mind.'

'1941. John GIELGUD holding up a skull.'

The exercise was designed both to designate the gaps in individual and theatre history; the silences and subversions as well as the notion of the play's history, within and beyond history. How far is any representation of *Hamlet* a postponed presentation of its own times? Or rather, as Hamlet more eloquently comments, 'The time is out of joint. Oh curséd spite that I was born to set it right.' The exercise puts experience inside and outside time; but it also builds meaning as a community of signifiers, traces, spectres. Meaning, like life, is always on the move. Related exercises might involve memorable date, place, and time for any text, experience, or issue. Again a degree of anonymity is recommended at the outset to avoid excessive anchorage in self-identity. Random mis-identifications make for better mutual learning and they are simply more fun. (The deconstructive temper is sportive!) In terms of the rich omnipresence of drama in life David Booth summarises the myriad-minded impact of these interrelated traces of memory:

> We are entertained, informed, angered, persuaded, manipulated, or touched, both consciously and subliminally, by thousands of per-formances we experience, and sometimes we are changed because of their influence and their impact on our lives. (Gallagher and Booth, 2003, p 18)

The notion of a tragic, violent society was carried through to the final day's work, both in the practice observation and the research station. Just as we had traveled through history, world and individual, in our versions of *Hamlet, Antigone*, totalitarian society and subjectivities, so we would move beyond the conference and back again to notions of performance and power; the *violence of representation*. In terms of the wider conference programme we also discussed John O'Toole's 'Research Conversation' at the conference on mental illness and doc-toral work. In terms of *Hamlet* we debated male and female mad-ness; we discussed and deconstructed the ambiguous notion of 'method in madness' – a link back to the work of the day before ('making rules'.) The research station also responded to Jonothan Neelands' work on *acts of violence*. The work involved portraying our own fears (of deconstruction, for example) as 'scarecrows' that, in a later stage of the seminar were to be destroyed or concealed, 'got rid of' somewhere in the room. Was post-structuralism the monster that would engulf our capacity to hold on to structure and stable mean-ing? By what violence were the norms of society disrupted/enforced by a community of meaning? We then set out to re-discover our scarecrows *after* hearing the announcement of a real news item of *another* scarecrow episode of anxiety, fear and violence:

October 10, 1998. Gay Man beaten and Left for Dead; 2 are charged

> By James Brooke. Laramie, Wyo., Oct 9 – At first the passing bi-cyclist thought the crumpled form lashed to a ranch fence was a scarecrow. But when he stopped, he found the burned, battered and nearly lifeless body of Matthew Shepard, an open gay college student who had been tied to the fence 18 hours earlier.

My sense here was (in Judith Thompson's words) 'sometimes out of this theatre of power in the classroom arises a harrowing drama' (cited in Gallagher and Booth, 2003, p31). As tutor I had missed the Stratford performance of *Richard III* the previous evening and instead had spoken at a county-wide police-community initiative on homophobic bullying in schools, linked to a screening of the Laramie Project, a play/film based on a documentary drama research concerning the news item above. I note David Booth's statement that 'We need to continually remind ourselves of the complex and different contexts that allow us to enter the 'as if, what if' world' (Gallagher and Booth, 2003, p 17). My justification also reflected what Ellis defined as deconstruction's mode of operation: 'Formulations are chosen not for their logical or intellectual appropriateness but, instead, for their drama and shock. Extremes of formulation are thus required' (1989, pp 141-2). The lost scarecrow is not the same as the one 'discovered'; nor can one that has been torn up, lost or destroyed be brought back to its original form. What had seemed like a release from the scarecrow was now re-embodied in fragments, or haunted each of us as a spectre of its former self. The research station cannot be adequately described from this point on, since 'a single theatre performance can never be replicated, for its effect is determined by such a list of variables that each occasion will hold a unique experience' (Gallagher and Booth, 2003, p 19).

Research station activity shifted from the monstrous 'event' to grotesque representations – how do we classify the monstrous, the marginal, the outsider? How do we keep the margins on the margins, at a distance? The deconstructive position aims to show the monster within that constitutes our sense of the normal. 'Monster' comes from *monstrare* (to exhibit, display) and *monere* (to warn, a portent) and these features seem to be central to the ambiguous interventions entertained by the deconstructive project, with supplementary roots elsewhere in Heathcote's 'signs and portents'. The failure of categories to make sense is the condition for the possibility of those things that we can classify using words and concepts. The notion of violent hierarchies therefore constitutes representation itself. Questions focused on the dead end which deconstruction had led us to; a madness or monstrosity beyond language itself, yet constitutive of sense and structure.

'Methodological' assessment

Deconstruction inhabits philosophy in a fashion similar to the virus that multiplies and mutates in its host's body. We deploy blocks, boxes, barriers, but deconstruction undermines them by constantly re-inventing itself, by always being for mutability and meta-morphosis. Its project cannot be adequately expressed in terms of a *bricolage* or 'tool-box' or even a repertoire of tricks. If it could be reduced, then it could be identified, classified, eradicated, frozen in its tracks. If genre, for instance, is most fascinating in its moments of mutation, so deconstruction comes to life between chaos and struc-ture, at the limit, in the hybrid, in the unique traces of singularity, rather than totalised systems of order and power that are *closed* to playful performance. None the less, the inner tensions of the deconstructive project were constantly undermining the notion of delivering a product, a tangible outcome or a set of transferable skills. The spectre of soft, mass-market deconstruction crosses the stage, or the temptation and danger of what Christopher Norris has called 'assimilating deconstruction to a vague thematics of textual am-bivalence and 'self-reflexivity'' (1989, p 167). Helpfully he proceeds to admit 'Yet the fact remains that Derrida's chosen texts are those which more or less explicitly thematise the deconstructive logic at work within them' (1989, p 168).

Yet there was a nagging sense that if one grasps what is constituted by deconstruction, then it has already slipped through your hands or vanished off stage, as intangible as a spectre. The charge of improper or reductive simplification is often levelled at Derrida's followers and explicators. One example will suffice, John M. Ellis writing an assess-ment of Jonathan Culler: 'On the one hand, Culler has a gift for ex-pounding difficult ideas; on the other hand, he 'domesticates' them and removes their challenging, difficult quality.' (1989, p 149). Ellis's book, *Against Deconstruction*, is excellent if you read it against itself, or transfer its inner logic and judgements to performance. I note his sense of deconstruction's slippery deception that exists alongside a sense that 'The moves made in the typical deconstructive perfor-mance are sufficiently regular that they can be schematised' (*ibid* p 137). If his statement is correct then the possibility of a methodology might be facilitated, even made present, framed within the research station, open for public viewing. At the other extreme was something altogether more chaotic, 'The promise of a full-scale totalising *method* is undone by the inbuilt tendency of signifying systems to create paradoxical effects and conflicts of meaning which admit of no ultimate resolution' (Norris, 1989, p 165).

Post-structuralism is fatally fascinated by the singularity of the performance event in all its rich and hard-earned uniqueness. Post-structuralism is at home in those moments when meaning is most elusively forged – with a delightful undecidability rather than unreadability. Deconstruction is not just textual; it is contextual, even out of context. In deconstructive terms, for instance, an 'example' is something taken *out of* a larger context. It is also rather ambiguously a precedent and a prototype; both a traditional and an innovatory model. In deconstructing 'story' and 'history' Derrida offers the possibility of recovering histories that have been 'repressed', 'minoritised', 'deligitimated'. In part then, the project is a political one. Deconstruction is Janus-faced and paradoxical; it looks two ways at once: the 'text as world' and the 'world as text'. As Derrida says:

> I do not 'concentrate' in my reading ... either exclusively or primarily on those points that appear to be the most 'important', 'central', 'crucial'. Rather, I deconcentrate, and it is the secondary, eccentric, lateral, marginal, parasitic, borderline cases which are 'important' to me and are the source of many things, such as pleasure, but also insight into the general functioning of a textual system. (1988, p 44)

In summary, deconstructive strategy often takes something marginal or peripheral, in order to disrupt what seems most settled at the centre. It is, therefore, a space of hypercritical and hyper-creative renewal, based on what was always, already there. Deconstruction also frequently employs parody and pastiche. It is parasitic upon the texts it reads. This may involve miming performances; sampling; supplementing and even supplanting them in a fashion that appears rather disrespectful. The business is to tease out the unacknowledged ideological assumptions at the level of signifiers. Within the broad field of post-structuralist approaches, deconstruction is itself a *slippery* performance for all involved. That is why it is an exciting journey, without origin, without destination.

Conclusion

At the end of the conference, members of the research station delivered a presentation of their work. They employed recorded voices of absent members of the group, on tape and mobile, as well as fragments of concepts, key words and themes, that took on a shifting life as they were re-positioned or re-presented on the projection screen. The sampling of 'meaning' (cutting up, joining, pastiche, parody) suggested the unfinished project of modernity; also the sense that we are doomed to shuffle concepts we can never erase; our ears straining after distant voices and spectral visions. The research station's compilation of words was a fitting gift of deconstructive signs that ask to be read in any order, for they unfold many stories.

monstrare to monster lies MASTER scary -ions Leader from impossible ANSWERS DON'T It QUEST is NOT QUITE (under) to warn confusing IN THE TRUTH Refreshing Slave DE TRUTH CONSTRUCTION is (ground) (pulled) TRUTH genres (from) FOLLOW THE *monere* IN THE TRUTHS (up) WHO's NOT show QUITE WHOSE mix comes not to (shifting) WHOO!

Recommended Reading

The most accessible short guides are those by Appignanesi and Collins listed below. For applications to theatre see Carlson, Fortier, and Gallagher. Counter arguments can be found in the texts by Ellis and Washington.

Reference

Appignanesi, Richard and Chris Garratt (1999) *Introducing Postmodernism*, Cambridge, Icon Books

Bolton, Gavin (1998) *Acting in Classroom Drama: a critical analysis*, Stoke on Trent, Trentham Books

Carlson, Marvin (1996) *Performance: a critical introduction*, London and New York, Routledge

Collins, Jeff and Bill Mayblin (2000) *Introducing Derrida*, Cambridge, Icon Books

Derrida, Jacques (1988) *Limited Inc*, Northwestern University Press

Ellis, John M. (1989) *Against Deconstruction*, Princeton, Princeton University Press

Ellmann, Richard, (1984) *James Joyce*, Oxford, Oxford University Press

Fortier, Mike (1997) *Theory/Theatre*, London and New York, Routledge

Gallagher, Kathleen and David Booth [Eds] (2003) *How Theatre Educates: Convergences and Counterpoints with Artists, Scholars and Advocates*, Toronto, Buffalo and London, University of Toronto Press

Norris, Christopher (1989) *The Deconstructive Turn: essays in the rhetoric of philosophy*, London and New York, Routledge

O'Neill, Cecily (1995) *Drama Worlds: A Framework for Process Drama*. Portsmouth, NH, Heinemann

Washington, Peter (1989) *Fraud: Literary Theory and the End of English*, London, Fontana Press

Index